Daniel's Difficulties Resolved

Revelation's Secrets Revealed

Daniel's Difficulties Resolved

—

Revelation's Secrets Revealed

By
Roderick L Yip M.D.

TEACH Services, Inc.

Copyright © 2004 TEACH Services, Inc.
ISBN 978-1-57258-277-4
Library of Congress Control Number: 2004104752

Published by

TEACH Services, Inc.
www.TEACHServices.com

Contents

PREFACE

It is with great hesitation that I approach a work of this magnitude knowing that greater minds than mine have grappled with and explored these magnificent books—Daniel and The Revelation.

It is not my intention to deal with either Daniel or The Revelation in a comprehensive way. I will seek to clarify selected areas of difficulty knowing that valid differences of opinion will arise from which all, including myself, can profit by our willingness to listen to each other.

In approaching this study I make no apology for using Isa. 28:9, 10 as the basis for understanding these books. "Whom shall he teach knowledge? And whom shall he make to understand doctrine? Them that are weaned from the milk, and drawn from the breast. For precept must be upon precept, precept upon precept; line upon line, line upon line; here a little, and there a little."

Ellen White repeatedly endorses the precept upon precept, line upon line approach to Bible study, especially as it relates to doctrine. This method of study has been disparagingly called the "proof text" method of study. "Intellectuals" have advocated the contextual method of study. The contextual method of study can lead to erroneous ideas of doctrine. For example, the vast majority of the Christian world believes in an immortal soul. They read Eccl. 12:7, "Then shall the dust return to the earth as it was and the Spirit shall return unto God who gave it." After reading a few verses before and after, they claim proof of an immortal soul—life immediately after death. Is this not the "proof text" method where one text is read in the context of verses before and

vii

after, and conclusions are drawn? This method is dangerous and should be used with great caution in arriving at doctrine.

We see greater wisdom in looking at Eccl. 9:5, 6, "For the living know that they shall die, but the dead know not anything…" Job 14:21, "His sons come to honor and he knoweth it not," Ps. 115:17, "The dead praise not the Lord," and so forth.

Some may say, the Isa. 28:9, 10 method can also be misused such as putting Gen. 4:8 "…Cain rose up against Abel his brother, and slew him," with Luke 10:37 (last part), "…go and do thou likewise." This type of far out reasoning demeans the credibility of those using it.

This is not to say, that looking at the context surrounding a given text is without value. But God has given us the precept upon precept method to safeguard His church from arriving at false doctrine, prevalent in the world today.

We pray for the Holy Spirit to enlighten our minds as we use the method given us in Isa. 28:9, 10, and endorsed by the prophetic gift, to arrive at a proper understanding of the word of God.

It should be mentioned here that the word "Section" will be used in this book in the place of "Chapter" to designate the divisions of this work. This is to avoid confusion when reference is made to another part of the work. "Section" will apply to the divisions in these books. "Chapters" will refer to the divisions in the books of Daniel and The Revelation.

DANIEL'S DIFFICULTIES RESOLVED

SECTION 1

FORMAT OF THE BOOKS OF DANIEL AND THE REVELATION

This exciting book—The Book of Daniel—is composed of a historical part and a prophetic part. The historical part embraces chapter 1 and chapters 3–6. Chapter 2 and 7–12 cover the prophetic part of the book.

We will not be considering the historical part of the book. It provides interesting reading. It gives straight forward information of facts not requiring interpretation.

The prophetic parts of Daniel must be seen in its four great repeats of the theme, Babylon, Medo-Persia, Greece and Rome. In the last two repeats of the theme, Babylon is omitted. With each repeat of the theme, more information is given. This is God's way of not only giving us more information, but also, by repetition, He cements the concepts in our thinking.

In Dan. 2, Babylon, Medo-Persia, Greece and Rome are represented by the great image of Nebuchadnezzar's dream. In Dan. 7, the same kingdoms are represented by four diverse beasts, the lion, the bear, the leopard and the dreadful and terrible beast. In Dan. 8 and 9, Babylon is omitted. In Dan. 8, Medo-Persia, Grecia and Rome are represented by the ram, the he-goat and the little horn which grew to be exceeding great. In Dan. 10, 11, and 12, Babylon is omitted. The angel details history from Darius the Mede, Medo-Persia, through Greece, Rome, France, and to our day.

1

We see a similar format in the book of Revelation, where there are three great repeats of the theme—the true church, the apostasy (or the false church coming out of the true church) and God's judgments on the apostasy. These we know as the seven churches, the seven seals and the seven trumpets. The second repeat is seen in Rev. 12—the pure woman clothed with the sun—the true church. This is followed by the apostasy of Rev. 13—the leopard beast and the lamb-like beast—the United States in prophecy. We have an insert of the three angels messages, then God's judgments on the apostasy covered in Rev. 14–16.

The third repeat of the theme, as in Daniel, omits the true church. It starts with the apostasy—the harlot woman of Rev. 17 and is followed by God's judgment on the apostasy and the end of the world covered in chapters 18–20. Chapters 21 & 22 pictures the renewal of all things. Any reading of Revelation as a sequence from chapters 1–22 represents a failure to see the repeated themes of this great and exciting book.

It should be pointed out that Jesus' Matt. 24 discourse on the history of the world follows this method of repeating and enlarging the concept. For instance, Jesus first sequence starts in His day and proceeds to verse 14 where the gospel of the kingdom is preached to the entire world and then the end comes. The second sequence (or repeat) starts with a going back to the destruction of Jerusalem in verse 15—the abomination of desolation standing in the Holy place, and ends with verse 27 with "as the lightening cometh from the east and shineth even to the west, so shall the coming of the Son of Man be." The third sequence (repeat) goes back to time immediately after the tribulation of those days (days of papal persecution), and ends with Jesus saying that no one knows when the day or the hour of His appearing would be (verse 36). The fourth repeat begins with the people of the last days being as in the days of Noah (verse 37), and ends with a warning to be ready for no man knows the hour of His coming (verse 44). Verses 45–51 contrasts the blessing of His faithful servants with the eternal loss of the evil servants.

It should be pointed out that the tribulation mentioned by Jesus in Matt. 24:21 and 29 should not be confused with the time of trouble mentioned in Dan. 12:1.

The tribulation mentioned by Jesus is the tribulation of His church—the 1260 years of Papal persecution. Notice that He said that "immediately after the tribulation of those days shall the sun be darkened, and the moon shall not give her light..." These events are in the past.

In contrast to that, Dan. 12:1 indicates that Michael stands up; probation is closed. Then there shall be a time of trouble such as never was since there was a nation. The close of probation and the great time of trouble among the nations is yet in the future. The two should not be confused.

The repeated themes in both the books of Daniel and The Revelation need to be kept in mind for a proper grasp of the messages of the books.

SECTION 2

PRINCIPLES OF INTERPRETATION

Before delving into the difficulties of Daniel and The Revelation, certain principles of interpretation need to be stated and understood.

PRINCIPLE #1

We need to keep in mind the repeated themes seen in the structure of the book. (See section 1)

PRINCIPLE #2

When an interpretation is given in the text itself as in Dan. 2:36–45, we must put aside our biases, pay attention to what is said (written) and our understanding of the matter must match as closely as possible to what is said.

PRINCIPLE #3

This principle is allied to principle number two. There are a number of instances in both the books of Daniel and The Revelation where the angel speaks. For instance, "Gabriel makes this man to understand the vision (Dan. 8:16)," "And now I will show thee the truth," Dan. 11:2. "I will tell thee the mystery of the woman, and of the beast that carrieth her..." Rev. 17:7. Whenever these statements appear and the angel speaks, we must put aside all preconceived biases, pay close attention to the words of the angel and your understanding of the prophecy must match what the angel declares the prophecy to be. If your understanding does not match the angel's words, you may be adding or taking away from the prophecy for which serious consequences are stated in Rev. 22:18, 19.

PRINCIPLE #4

Similar words, phrases and sentences appearing in these books may focus on the same event, as the spokes of a wheel point to the hub. Similar words, phrases and sentences may enlighten us as to a given subject without it being the hub itself.

PRINCIPLE #5

God may call our attention to a subject in one part of the book, but may not describe that subject until later in the book. For example, Babylon is first mentioned in Rev. 14, but is not described until Rev. 17. Waters are mentioned in Rev. 13 but again, not described until Rev. 17. The "third part" is mentioned again and again in Rev. 8 & 9, but insight is not given on this issue until Rev. 16. Understanding the three parts of Rev. 16 helps us to determine who the "third part" is. This also enlightens us as to who the "fourth part" is, as mentioned in Rev. 6.

We need to keep in mind that the book of Daniel is largely a political history of the world from 600 years BC to the climatic end time. The book of The Revelation is largely a religious history of the Christian church from apostolic days to the end time.

PRINCIPLE #6

There are clues in the book of Daniel that are essential to the understanding of parts of The Revelation. They are not readily seen and are easily overlooked in a casual reading of Daniel. Uriah Smith unlocks these clues. We can then apply them to the understanding of difficult portions of Revelation.

PRINCIPLE #8

Above all we should always keep in mind that both the books of Daniel and The Revelation focus on Jesus and His second coming.

SECTION 3

DANIEL 2

Dan. 2, the first sequence of Babylon, Medo-Persia, Greece and Rome, is a simple clear-cut delineation of the political history of the world from about 600 BC to the climatic end of time.

There are little difficulties to be found in this chapter. We have no problem linking the great empires of the world with the gold, silver, brass and iron of Nebuchadnezzar's dream. We are told what the stone which destroyed the image represents. And the dream is certain, and the interpretation thereof sure.

Significant statements in this chapter occur in verse 28, where God is telling Nebuchadnezzar and us "...what shall be in the latter days." Verse 29 speaks to Nebuchadnezzar of "...what shall come to pass." Or in other words, what shall come to pass in the latter days. God is revealing to Nebuchadnezzar what will transpire following his reign.

Daniel begins his interpretation of the dream with a bold, "Thou art this head of gold. And after thee shall arise another kingdom inferior to thee..."

What is not seen here, but is pointed out by Uriah Smith, is that five minor kings are omitted from the prophecy. They reigned between Nebuchadnezzar, and the Medo-Persian conquest under Cyrus. These are treated as "nobodies." The prophecy moves quickly from Nebuchadnezzar to Darius the Mede. This is significant information when seen in the light of Dan. 11 where nine minor kings are not listed in the prophecy between Xerxes and

6

Alexander the Great. (See comments on Dan. 11, section 8.) Using this clue of omitting the minor kings, we obtain a clear understanding of what the angel is saying in Rev. 17 in regards to the seven heads (seven kings—the major players) of the seven-headed, ten-horned beast. (See *Revelation's Secrets Revealed*)

Another significant statement is found in verse 34 where "…a stone was cut out without hands…" is mentioned. This is seen again in verse 45 where the stone cut out of the mountain "without hands" represents Christ's kingdom. Again in Dan. 8:25, speaking of Rome, the persecuting power will destroy wonderfully the mighty and the holy people and who will stand up against the Prince of Princes (Jesus Crucified). It says,"… He shall be broken 'without hand.'"

SECTION 4

DANIEL 7

Dan. 7 represents the second repeat of the theme Babylon, Medo-Persia, Greece and Rome. The symbols used here are the lion, the bear, the leopard and the dreadful and terrible fourth beast of verse seven.

Of interest is the little horn of the fourth beast, which uprooted three of the original 10 horns of the divided Roman Empire. These uprooted horns (or powers) were the Vandals, the Heruli and the Ostragoths.

Attention should be called to the difference between the little horn of this chapter, and the little horn of Dan. 8. The little horn of Dan. 7 comes up <u>after</u> the division of the Roman Empire into its ten parts and destroys three of the ten in order to establish itself. That little horn will speak great words against the Most High; it will persecute God's people; it will attempt to change God's law. This is definitely the Papal Roman power as is confirmed by the last part of Dan. 7:25. This little horn will have power over God's people for a "…time, and times, and the dividing of times." Most Bible students know that this refers to the 1260 days of Papal dominance existing from 538 AD to 1798 AD This time period is so important, that it is referred to twice in Daniel and five times in The Revelation.

On the other hand, the little horn of Dan. 8 comes up at the latter end of the Greek Empire, when "…the transgressors are come to the full…," or when the Jewish nation was about to fill its cup of iniquity. See Dan. 8:23. Remember Jesus' words to

8

Jerusalem just before His death, "... Your house is left unto you desolate." The Jews would fill their cup of iniquity by putting Jesus to death.

The little horn of Dan. 8 is the beginnings of the Roman Empire. It started at the demise of the Greek Empire as a little horn a small power which grew and "...waxed exceeding great..." (More details on this in comments on Dan. 8)

It is of interest to notice three verses in Dan. 7 in regards to the mouth of the little horn. Verse 8 of chapter 7 says, that he had a mouth that spake great things. Verse 20 says, that he had a mouth that spake "...very great things." Verse 25 says, "...He shall speak great words against the Most High..." Revelation finalizes the picture by saying he had a mouth "...speaking great things and blasphemies." Rev. 13:5.

Another important concept that should not be over looked is found in Dan. 7:11. Daniel was looking and saw "...even till the beast was slain, and his body destroyed, and given to the burning flame." The fourth beast is Rome, and God pictures Rome as existing until He destroys it in "...the burning flame." How is Rome considered to exist till Jesus puts an end to it in "the burning flame?" As one puts it, "Rome is Pagan until it becomes Papal." They are one and the same although under two different disguises. See *Great Controversy* p. 579 and 2 Thess. 2:3–8 which confirm that the Papacy will exist till Jesus puts an end to it.

Looking at Dan. 7:13, do not let the words "...one like the Son of Man came with the clouds of heaven" cause you to link this with the second coming. The rest of the verse says, He came to the Ancient of Days—that is to God the Father. The reason is given in verse 14 where He receives from the Father dominion, glory and a kingdom.

This is in keeping with Jesus' parable of the nobleman who went into a far country to receive for himself a kingdom and to return (Luke 19:12). Luke 19:15 states that the nobleman returned after having received the kingdom. In other words Jesus receives the kingdom from His Father before He returns at His second coming.

The focus of the books of Daniel and The Revelation is on the second coming of our Lord.

SECTION 5

DANIEL 8

Dan. 8 and 9 are the third repeat of the theme of successive world empires. Babylon is omitted. Dan. 8 & 9 are one. Dan. 8 has been the problem chapter in many ways. One reason for the problem is that commentators start interpreting the vision given in verses 1–14 without paying close attention to what the angel Gabriel is saying. In verse 16, a voice is heard between the banks of Ulai saying, "Gabriel make this man to understand the vision."

As Gabriel interprets the vision in Dan. 8:18–26, we notice that there is no word mentioned concerning "sanctuary," "offerings," "sacrifices," nor a "false priesthood." True, there is a false sanctuary (or church) with a false priestly system and so forth, but that concept cannot be deduced from any portion of Gabriel's explanation of Dan. 8. If we follow Gabriel's explanation of the vision, he starts with stating that the ram is Media and Persia, the rough goat is Greece, the great horn between his eyes is the first king—Alexander the Great, the horn is broken and for it came up four horns—the four divisions of the Greek Empire under the rule of Ptolemy, Selucus, Lysemicus and Cascander.

Verse 23 states that at the latter time of their kingdom, or towards the end of the Greek Empire, "…when transgressors are come to the full…" or when the Jewish nation would finally fill their cup of iniquity, (see Matt. 23:34–38) a king of fierce countenance shall "stand up"—or take the kingdom to rule. This king of fierce countenance is Rome which developed from the western division of the Greek Empire and spread, as verse 9

11

points out, towards the South, the East and towards the pleasant land, or Palestine.

The rest of Gabriel's comments on the work of the "king of fierce countenance" or the little horn of Dan. 8 (the development of the Roman Empire), is remarkable for the absence of sanctuary images.

Many commentators on Dan. 8 spend a lot of time expounding on the true sanctuary in heaven, contrasting it with the false Papal system, and being influenced by such words appearing in the text of the vision such as, "sanctuary," "sacrifice," "daily," "transgression" and so forth.

We notice that Gabriel's explanation of the work of the little horn appearing in verses 24 and 25 almost exclusively deals with its power to destroy, "...and he shall destroy wonderfully... and shall destroy the mighty and the holy people... and by peace shall destroy many; He shall also stand up against the Prince of Princes..." The persecuting practice of Rome, the martyring of God's people and the crucifixion of the Son of God, the Prince of Princes, is clearly referred to in these verses. Little more is said concerning the vision by Gabriel.

With Gabriel's words in mind, we now turn back to the details of the vision. The vision of Dan. 8 occurred two years after the vision of Dan. 7. Daniel saw a ram (Medo-Persia) pushing westward, northward and southward. This ram, Medo-Persia, came from the East. Persia is to the East.

Daniel then saw a he-goat coming from the West. The he-goat (Greece) is located west of Palestine. It traveled rapidly towards the ram, cast the ram to the ground and stamped upon him. The imagery here of the he-goat stamping on the ram is to convey to us the idea of Greece conquering and destroying Medo-Persia. Concerning the "notable horn between his eyes," the first king (Alexander the Great), the prophecy stated that when he was strong he would be broken. Alexander died at a relatively young age after conquering Medo-Persia. Thereafter four "notable" ones, or horns, would succeed Alexander's rulership. These would occupy the "four winds of heaven," or would dominate the kingdom, East, West, North and South.

The vision showed that out of one of them, probably the Western division would arise a little horn which would wax "exceeding great" towards the South, the East and toward the pleasant land, Palestine.

The concept of the "little horn" of Dan. 8 is different from the "little horn" of Dan. 7. (See section 4 on Dan. 7). The little horn of Dan. 7 comes into existence after the division of the Roman Empire into its ten parts. The Papacy, (the little horn of Dan. 7), rooted out three of the original ten divisions, the Vandals, the Heruli and the Ostragoths as it established its supremacy.

The little horn of Dan. 8 should be looked upon as a horn, or power, starting with small beginnings and waxing, or growing gradually to be "exceeding great." This concept fits into the history of the development of the Roman Empire. We notice that Babylon was overthrown in a night. Today, Babylon; tomorrow, Medo-Persia. Medo-Persia was overthrown by Greece at the Battle or Arbela. Again, as it were, today, Medo-Persia; tomorrow, Greece. Rome came to power by no specific overnight battle. By assisting various groups fighting their enemies, Rome gradually dominated the countries she assisted, Egypt at first; Palestine, then countries to the North and East. Eventually Rome made vassals of these countries taxing them for the protection she afforded them. Thus the wording "…a little horn, which waxed (or grew) to be "exceeding great." It is here appropriate to point out that Medo-Persia was "great" (verse 4). Greece was "very great" (verse 8). Rome, the little horn waxed "exceeding great" (verse 9). This represents the relative power and greatness of the three.

The little horn "waxed great" even to the host of heaven. How do we understand this? Can developing Rome have any contact with the stars of heaven, if "host" refers to stars? Unlikely. Can Rome have any contact with angels or beings of unfallen worlds if "host" refers to these? No. Then we must look for a more logical meaning for the words "host of heaven." We go to Josh. 5:14 where Joshua meets a man with his sword drawn. "Are you for us or for our adversaries? Nay, but as captain of the 'host' of the Lord am I come." This is a clear reference to His people.

The little horn (Rome) would cast some of God's host (God's people) to the ground. He would cast some of the "stars" to the ground. Who are the stars? Not the fiery orbs revolving around God's throne in His mighty universe, but the leaders of God's people. Look at Rev. 1:20, where Jesus says, the seven stars in His right hand are the "angels" of the seven churches. These are not literal angels, but the leaders of the seven churches. Jesus is not reproving angels, but the leaders of the seven churches when He says, for instance, unto the <u>angel</u> of the church of Ephesus writes….. "Because thou hast left thy first love." Unto the <u>angel</u> of the church of Thyatira write…. Thou sufferest that woman Jezebel… to teach and seduce my servants," and so forth. We see here stars in Jesus hands are angels and the leaders of the seven churches. The little horn cast some of the host (God's people) and some of the stars (the leaders of His people) to the ground and stamped upon them. This is a symbolic representation of persecution.

Notice the similarity of the terminology used to indicate destruction of. In verse 7, Greece (he-goat) cast the ram (Medo-Persia) to the ground and stamped upon him and destroyed him. In verse 10, the little horn cast some of the host and of the stars (God's people and their leaders) to the ground and stamped upon them. Destruction or persecution is indicated here.

It may be wise to state at this point that another term is used in scripture to convey the idea of stamping upon to destroy. That term is "trodden under foot." We see this term used in Dan. 8:13. It carries the same meaning there as casting to the ground and stamping upon them. This term is also seen in Rev. 11:2 where the Holy City (God's people) will be trodden under foot for 42 months—the 1260 years of Papal persecution.

Dan. 8:11 tells us that the little horn will magnify himself even to the Prince of the host. Gabriel tells us that he shall also stand up against the Prince of Princes. It was the little horn (Rome) who was responsible for the actual crucifixion of Jesus. In standing up against the Prince of Princes, Gabriel's next statement is that he shall be "broken without hand." It will be the kingdom of the Prince of Princes that will finally destroy Rome. This is one of several statements that indicate that God considers Rome to exist until He puts an end to it.

The rest of Dan. 8:11 has been a problem for many. Uriah Smith gives us noteworthy clues to understanding the messages of verses 11 & 13.

First, what is meant by the "daily sacrifice?" to understand the meaning of the "daily sacrifice," we go to verse 13 where the question is raised "…how long shall be the vision concerning the daily sacrifice, and the transgression of desolation, to give both the sanctuary and the host to be trodden under foot?"

We need to look at how the scriptures use the word "desolation." What does desolation mean? Isa. 54:1 says, "Sing O barren, thou that didst not bear; break forth into singing, and cry aloud, thou that didst not travail with child: for more are the children of the desolate (those without Christ) than the children of the married wife, saith the Lord." This corresponds with the wide and narrow gate of Jesus teachings.

Look at Jer. 2:12, 13, "Be astonished, O ye heavens, at this, and be horribly afraid, be ye very desolate saith the Lord. For my people have committed two evils; they have forsaken Me the fountain of living waters, and hewed them out cisterns, broken cisterns, that can hold no water."

Jer. 12:10, 11 says, "Many pastors have destroyed my vineyard, they have trodden my portion under foot (destroyed it). They have made my pleasant portion a desolate wilderness. They have made it desolate, and being desolate, it mourneth unto Me; the whole land is made desolate, because no man layeth it to heart."

In Matt. 23:38 Jesus, speaking to Jerusalem who rejected Him says, "Behold your house is left unto you <u>desolate</u>." In other words, Jesus was about to reject the Jews as His chosen people. A person, a church, a nation without Christ is spoken of as being <u>desolate</u>.

Now let us go back to Dan. 8:13. The Papal system is spoken of as the "transgression of desolation." In Dan. 11:31 and Dan. 12:11 the term "abomination that maketh desolate" is used. By transgressions and by abominations she became desolate of Christ.

The Papacy began as a part of the Christian faith. In 2 Thess. 2, Paul speaks of the falling away and the development of the man of sin. As time went on, the Papal system by transgressions and abominations became desolate of Christ, hence the terms transgression of "desolation" or "abomination of desolation," as Jesus speaks of Rome in an all inclusive fashion in Matt. 24.

How does this insight fit into Dan. 8:13? The transgression of desolation is Papal Rome. What is the so called "daily sacrifice?" As most Bible students know, the word "sacrifice" is not in the ancient manuscripts, and therefore was probably not in the original. As Uriah Smith points out, the word "daily" should have been translated as "continual" or "continuance." This continual or continuance of desolation refers to Pagan Rome (never ever having Christ in it) continually desolate of Christ.

Now let us read the question raised in Dan. 8:13, and insert these concepts into the verse. "How long shall be the vision concerning the continuance and the transgression of desolation to give both the sanctuary and the host to be trodden under foot?"

The continuance and transgression of desolation—both "continuance" and transgression" modifies the word desolation. Continuance of desolation (Pagan Rome) and the transgression of desolation (Papal Rome) will cause the sanctuary and the host (God's people) to be trodden under foot. And the concept of persecution of God's people is consistent with Gabriel's explanation of the vision.

Another point that needs clarification is that "sanctuary and the host" of Dan. 8:13 refers to God's people. In Rev. 11:2, the term "Holy City" is used to refer to God's people who will be trodden under foot 40 and two months. In several places in the Old Testament, the people of God are spoken of as the "city of the Lord," the Zion of the Holy One. Isa. 60:14, "The holy people.... A city not forsaken." Isa. 62:12 "Thou shalt be called the city of righteousness" (Isa. 1:26). They call themselves of the Holy City (Isa. 48:2) and so forth.

The sanctuary and the host of Dan. 8:13 are to be understood as the holy city which would be trodden under foot by Pagan Rome (continuance of desolation) and Papal Rome (transgression of desolation).

The question of time "how long" raised by the two saints speaking in Dan. 8:13 is not answered by Dan. 8:14. Two saints speaking to each other raised the question of time. Pagan Rome and Papal Rome persecuted God's people for 1798 years. This time period ended when Berthier took the Pope prisoner in 1798. Dan. 8:14 was an exchange between the angel and Daniel concerning the 2300 day prophecy which started in 457 BC and ending in 1844 AD. The time period of the 2300 day prophecy is much broader than Pagan or Papal Roman persecution of God's people.

The question of "how long" of Dan. 8:13 has an echo as it were in Rev. 6:10. The closing of the fourth seal ends at the time of the beginning of the reformation. The fifth seal begins as persecution abates—the souls under the alter figuratively crying, "how long O Lord, Holy and True doest thou not judge and avenge our blood on them that dwell on the earth." They were told to rest awhile. Others would be martyred as they were before the end.

SECTION 6

DANIEL 9

Chapter 9 of Daniel is a continuance of chapter 8 the third repeat of the prophetic sequences of Daniel. Daniel's vision of chapter 8, the ram, the he-goat and the little horn was given in the third year of Belshazzar. See Dan. 8:1. Babylon was besieged by Cyrus in the third year of Belshazzar. Since chapter 9 was apparently written in the first year of Darius, the Mede (See Dan. 9:1) it appears that only a short time may have elapsed between the vision of chapter 8, and the explanation (of the 2300 day prophecy) given by Gabriel in chapter 9.

Daniel was praying earnestly that God would not defer His promise to have the Jews return to Jerusalem after the 70 years of captivity. God answered his prayer with another 70—the 70 week prophecy. It should be pointed out that the 2300 day prophecy was the only part of Daniel's previous vision that was not elaborated on by Gabriel. As Daniel heard of the terrible persecution of God's people by the little horn and the standing up against the Prince of Princes, he could no longer bear it. He fainted. The effect of the vision and its interpretation so affected the prophet that he was sick for a number of days thereafter.

In Dan. 8:26, Gabriel barely touched on the 2300 day prophecy of Dan. 8:14. The prophet fainted. Gabriel returned in chapter 9 in answer to the prayer of the prophet that God would not defer the promised restoration. God reassured Daniel in verse 25 that the promise would be fulfilled. There would be a commandment given to restore and rebuild Jerusalem.

Gabriel advised Daniel to "...understand the matter, and consider the vision." Which vision? The one given in chapter 8. Daniel said in the last verse of Dan. 8 "...I was astonished at the vision, but none understood it." What did Daniel not understand? The major part of the vision was explained to Daniel—the terrible work of the little horn. It made him sick. The only part of the vision that was not explained and thus not understood was the part dealing with the 2300 day prophecy.

Here is where Gabriel began—70 weeks are determined or "cut off" from the 2300 day prophecy. The assumption is made that both the 70-week prophecy and the 2300 day prophecy had a common beginning date.

Gabriel says, that 70 weeks are determined (or allotted) to thy people and the holy city (Jerusalem) to finish transgression (or for the Jews to fill their cup of iniquity) after which the Jews would be rejected, and to also make an end of sins (or sin offerings). Reconciliation for iniquity would be made by Christ sacrifice on the cross. "Everlasting righteousness" would be available through Christ. To seal up the vision would be to make it sure; to certify the interpretation. "To anoint the Most Holy," as Uriah Smith points out, the Hebrew does not apply this to people (living things), but to inanimate objects. It most likely points to the anointing of the heavenly sanctuary for the beginning of Jesus work there in our behalf. The earthly sanctuary was similarly anointed before it was put into use by Moses for the children of Israel.

Gabriel plainly states that from the going forth of the commandment to restore and rebuild Jerusalem unto the Messiah will be 7 weeks, 3 score and 2 weeks, or a total of 69 weeks. From that starting point (the commandment to restore and rebuild) would bring you to the Messiah. That commandment went forth in the autumn of 457 BC The Messiah was anointed 69 weeks later (a day for a year) in AD 27.

After the 69th week (on the 70th week), the Messiah would be cut off. The crucifixion is referred to here. Verse 27 states that in the midst of the 70th week, the Messiah would cause the sacrifice and oblations to cease. How do we know that Jesus was crucified in the midst of the week (a day for a year)? Jesus was baptized at the end of the 69th week or AD 27. Thereafter, He attended 3 Passovers (a yearly Jewish feast). See John 2:13, John 5:1 and John 6:4. On the fourth Passover (recorded in John 13:1) it is recorded that Jesus knew that His hour was come. He was sacrificed for us, our Passover Lamb, at the fourth Passover, in the middle of the 70th week, just as the prophecy predicted.

The angel ended the explanation in chapter 9 by saying "...and for the overspreading of abominations, he shall make it desolate even until the consummation...." Because of the abominations of the Jewish nation Jesus would reject them, make them desolate, even to the time of the end—the consummation. What is determined will be poured out on the desolate. This is but one evidence of many that the Jewish nation is no longer, and will no longer be a part of God's plan to evangelize the world.

As a point of interest, it should be mentioned that Gabriel is mentioned by name only twice in the Old Testament. These two places are in Dan. 8 & 9. Gabriel is mentioned by name in the prophecy pointing to the Messiah. Gabriel is mentioned by name twice in the New Testament, and those two instances are in connection with the announcement of the forerunner of the Messiah and the birth of the Messiah.

SECTION 7

DANIEL 10

Thus far we have covered three of the four repeats of Daniel's prophecy. Nebuchadnezzar's image of Dan. 2 covers the basic series of Babylon, Medo-Persia, Greece and Rome. Dan. 7 elaborates on Babylon, Medo-Persia, Greece and Rome under the symbols of a lion, bear, leopard and a dreadful and terrible beast.

Dan. 8 & 9 (the third repeat) omits Babylon. It begins with Medo-Persia (the ram), Greece (the he-goat), and the small or little horn which waxed or grew to become exceeding great. Each of these repeats adds additional information to the prophecies preceding it.

Now we come to the fourth repeat in the series. This vision occurred in the third year of Cyrus. Chapters 10, 11 & 12 are one. Chapter 10 lists the circumstances which brought about the writing of this fourth sequence in the series.

In Dan. 8:27, Daniel says, he was astonished at the vision, but none understood it. This was in reference to the 2300-day prophecy, which was not explained until Gabriel returned to explain it in chapter 9.

Dan. 10:1 reveals a new vision. Daniel said of the vision he had, and his conversation with the angel, that he "...understood the thing and had understanding of the vision." Why then should we not understand the meaning of the vision?

Daniel was "mourning" for three weeks. He ate no pleasant bread, he drank no wine, and he ate no flesh for a full three weeks. On the 24th day of the first month, he sees a vision. He sees a man clothed with linen with his loins girded with fine gold. He had eyes as lamps of fire and arms and feet like polished brass his voice was as the voice of a multitude. Who is this person? In Rev. 1:13–15 John describes "…one like unto the Son of Man (Jesus) clothed with a garment down to the foot. He wore a golden girdle, His eyes were as a flame of fire and His feet like unto fine brass, His voice as the sound of many waters." It seems unavoidable to conclude that Daniel is seeing Jesus, the Son of Man.

Daniel describes his physical condition while in vision. This ends at verse 9. In verse 10, "…a hand touched me…" This was the hand of the angel. He said to Daniel that from the first day that he set his heart to understand, that the words of Daniel were heard, and that he came because of Daniel's words. Or in other words he came to give Daniel understanding.

However, the Prince of the kingdom of Persia (Cyrus) withstood the angel for 21 days. Apparently Cyrus was resisting the angel's influence in something that is not fully evident from the text. It could be his role issuing the command to restore and rebuild Jerusalem.

The angel said "… but, lo, Michael, one of the chief Princes (Jesus) came to help me." The angel then states his mission to Daniel. He came to inform Daniel as to what shall befall his people in the latter days.

In verse 16, the scene again shifts to the Son. "…one like the similitude of the Sons of Men touched my lips."

Daniel speaks. He said to one standing by, "how can I speak when there is neither strength nor breath in me?" Then one like the appearance of a man (the angel) touched Daniel and strengthens him. He addressed Daniel with that heavenly endearing compliment a "…man greatly beloved." The angel strengthens Daniel. Daniel responds by saying "Let my Lord speak; for thou hast strengthened me."

The angel then responds with, "Do you know why I have come to thee?" That information is forthcoming in chapter 11.

The angel says, "...now will I return to fight with the prince of Persia." As Uriah Smith points out, the angel is not fighting against the king of Persia, He is fighting with (side by side) supporting the king of Persia."...And when I am gone forth," (when he no longer supports Persia), "...lo, the Prince of Greece shall come." When heaven determines that Persia will end, the Greek Empire begins. Dan. 2:21 "...he removeth kings, and setteth up kings."

The angel ends the chapter by saying he will show Daniel that which is noted in the scripture of truth. He indicates that there is none "that holdeth with me in these things, but Michael your Prince." Only Michael and the angel are in the know of the things the angel was about to explain to the prophet.

SECTION 8

DANIEL 11

We need to keep in mind that chapters 10, 11 & 12 are one. This is the fourth and final repeat of the prophetic series in the book of Daniel.

Again Babylon is omitted. The angel starts by reminding Daniel that he was there to confirm and strengthen Darius the Mede. He supported Darius the Mede who was no longer. Cyrus was ruling when this vision was given. See Dan. 10:1. The angel outlines the history of the world from Medo-Persia to the end of time.

The Medo Persian empire is touched on in only two verses—Dan. 11:1, 2. The Greek Empire begins at verse 3, and ends at verse 19. Rome begins at verse 20 and goes through its Pagan phase, and its transformation to the Papal phase which receives the deadly wound at "the time of the end." As Uriah Smith points out, the "time of the end" is an appointed time when the 1260 years comes to an end. This ends at verse 35 where God's people will "fall to try them and to purge and to make them white, even to the time of the end." They will be persecuted till the "time of the end." The end of the 1260 years—a time appointed.

Verses 36–39 pictures France, the atheistic power that inflicted the deadly wound to Papal Rome, thus ending the 1260 years of Papal dominance and cruelty to God's people.

It is important to recognize that verses 36–39 refers to France and not to the Papacy as some have suggested. If we insist that verses 36–39 refers to the Papacy, then verses 40–45 that follows, will not make sense. It is for this reason that there is confusion in our ranks as to the king of the South fighting the king of the North at some future time at the end. We have simply cut off verses 40–45 from the sequence of the prophecy placing it at some indistinct unknown time in the future, we know not when. Are we not doing the same unreasonable thing the Evangelicals are doing, e.g. Cutting off the 70th week from the 69th week of the 70-week prophecy, placing it over 2000 years from the rest of the prophecy? More on this later.

Now that we have had an overview of Dan. 11, let us go back to some of the details and interesting points in the chapter.

The angel tells Daniel in verse 1 that when Darius the Mede ruled, he was there to confirm and strengthen him. At the time of the angel's visit Cyrus was the current ruler. (See Dan. 10:1). The angel said, "Now I will tell you the truth." There will be three kings following Cyrus, as rulers of Persia. These, as Uriah Smith points out are, Cambyses, Smerdis and Darius Hystaspes. A fourth one will be richer than the three put together—this king was Xerxes who was a fabulously wealthy king. He raised an army who Herodotus numbered as 5,283,220 men. See *Daniel & The Revelation* chapter 11 by Uriah Smith. Xerxes will "stir up all against the realm of Greece." There was an uprising of the Greek sector of the kingdom which Xerxes successfully put down after the brave Spartans were betrayed by traitors. See *Daniel & The Revelation* chapter 11 "Unrolling the Scroll"

Verse 2 ends the brief history of the Medo-Persian empire. A mighty king is introduced in verse 3. This is the first king of the Grecian Empire (Alexander the Great). Two points are of importance here. Uriah Smith points out that nine minor kings are omitted from the prophecy. These spanned the time between Xerxes and Alexander the Great. This is of vital importance when viewed in the light of Dan. 2, where Daniel tells Nebuchadnezzar, "thou art this head of gold, and after thee shall arise another kingdom..." Five minor kings are here omitted between Nebuchadnezzar and the Medo-Persian empire. This information is used in understanding and naming the kings represented by the seven heads of the seven-head ten-horned beast of Rev. 17. (See *Revelation Secrets Revealed* on chapter 17).

The second point to consider in verses 2 and 3 is the meaning of the phrase "... shall stand up." Verse 2 says, "...there shall stand up" yet three kings in Persia." Verse 3 says, "and a mighty king shall stand up." Verse 4 says, "and when he shall stand up...." What is the significance of this statement? When a king "stands up," he takes the kingdom to rule. In Dan. 12:1 when Michael stands up, He takes the kingdom to rule. He receives the kingdom from his Father. Probation is closed!

In Rev. 17 we have the opposite statement. The seven heads are seven mountains and are seven kings. Five are fallen (no longer standing up). They are in the past. One is, or is presently ruling, and the other is not yet come. (More on this in *Revelation's Secret's Revealed* where the kings can be named and the prophecy is perfect).

When the mighty king (Alexander the Great) shall stand up, his kingdom will be broken and divided towards the four winds of heaven. This corresponds to Dan. 8:8, when the great horn of the he-goat was broken, and four notable horns came up towards the four winds of heaven.

The four divisions of the Greek Empire were under the control of Lysimachus, Cassander, Seleucus and Ptolemy. Lysimachus fought and conquered the successors of Cassander. Lysimachus was then overthrown by Seleucus, to form what is referred to in the early verses of the chapter as the king of the North. Ptolemy and his descendents controlled Egypt and is referred to as the king of the South.

Verses 5–13 depict the wars between the kings of the North and South. It begins with Ptolemy Soter of the South, and Seleucus Nicator of the North. To avoid burdening the reader with a collection of strange names of Greek-Egyptian kings of the South, and Greek-Seleucid kings of the North, I will refer the reader to the excellent work by Uriah Smith on Dan. 11:5–14.

Rome first comes to view in verse 14 under the appellation of "…robbers of thy people…" Uriah's Smith's description of the rise of Rome is interesting. He says, "Small and weak at first, it grew in strength and vigor with marvelous rapidity, reaching out cautiously here and there to try its prowess and test its warlike arm until with consciousness of its power it boldly reared it head among the nations of the earth and seized with invisible hand the helm of affairs. Henceforth the name of Rome stands upon the page of history, destined for long ages to control the world and to exert a mighty influence among the nation even to the end of time."

Dan. 11:14 introduces Rome as the "robbers of thy people" as Rome enters history by assisting Egypt, the king or kingdom of the South. From verse 14–19 we have the increasing involvement of Rome with both the kings of the South and the kings of the North. (See Uriah Smith's commentary on these verses.)

We eventually come to verse 20 where Rome now controls the world. "Then shall stand up in his estate a raiser of taxes in the glory of the kingdom." This raiser of taxes is Caesar Augustus who is considered the first emperor of Rome. Rome was considered to be in the heights of its glory in the days of Caesar Augustus. He is the Roman emperor with the longest rule (41 years).

Luke records this taxing activity of Caesar Augustus in Luke 2:1. "And it came to pass in those days, that there went out a decree from Caesar Augustus, that all the world should be taxed." Luke 2:1–5 elaborates on the taxing of the world by Caesar Augustus.

Dan. 11:21 mentions a "vile person" who would succeed Caesar Augustus. This is Tiberius Caesar who history confirms as such. He would be ruling when the Prince of the covenant (Jesus) would be broken or crucified.

The schemes of the early Roman Empire are given following verse 21. We notice that in verse 28 "…his heart shall be against the holy covenant." Verse 30 mentions the "indignation against the holy covenant." Rome would be against God's people. Interestingly enough, in the latter portion of verse 30, Rome would "...have intelligence with them that forsake the holy covenant." 2 Thess. 2:7 is brought to mind where the mystery of iniquity was already at work in Paul's day. They who forsook the holy covenant will eventually connive with the civil Roman government.Verse 31 references the destruction of the sanctuary. "...They shall pollute the sanctuary of strength." Thereafter we see the transition of Pagan to Papal Rome. "...They ...shall take away the "daily sacrifice" (the continuance of desolation, Pagan Rome), and they shall place (or establish) the abomination that maketh desolate (Papal Rome). Pagan Rome is taken out of the way to make room for the establishment of the Papacy.

Dan. 11:32 presents the contrast between those who forsook the covenant and those who remained faithful. Those who did wickedly against the covenant, Rome would corrupt with flatteries. In contrast, the people who knew their God would be strong and do exploits, or accomplish his purposes.

Verse 33 states what some of these exploits would be: "They...shall instruct many." In so doing they shall "...fall by the sword and by flame, by captivity, and by spoil, many days." The "many days" includes the 1260 years of Papal persecution and maybe more when you include the persecution under Pagan rule.

Verse 34 says, that "... when they shall fall they shall be holpen (helped) with a little help." This corresponds to Jesus statement in Matt. 24:22 that "...except those days (the days of tribulation—the 1260 years of Papal persecution) should be shortened, there should no flesh be saved (nothing would be left alive of the church).

Verse 35 reiterates the prophecy of persecution. It will be "...to try them, and to purge, and to make them white, even to the time of the end." Persecution will continue until the time of the end. "Because it is yet for a time appointed." In other words the time of the end is a specific time beginning at the abatement of Papal persecution (1798).

As was mentioned before, it is vitally important to understand that verses 36–39 is speaking of France, the atheistic power who ended the 1260 years of Papal dominance.

In verse 36, France, during the French Revolution, became atheistic. The Pope was the number one figure representing Christianity, (false Christianity though that may be). He was taken captive by Berthier, and died a prisoner in France. France would do "according to his will" and magnify itself above every God. It would speak marvelous things against the God of gods. France would prosper "...till the indignation be accomplished." France would exist until the end. France would not regard the God of his fathers, he would not regard the desire of woman. The marriage relationships were disannulled, divorce made easy, polygamy allowed and the family units ruined. He would not "...regard any god." This would be an atheistic power. We are made to understand that modern communism had its origin in France. When religion was finally reinstated in France after three and a half years of atheistic government, communism fled to the East where it apparently flourished in Russia.

In verse 38, France would honor the God of forces. At this time Napoleon had subjugated by force of arms all of Europe except England. France, besides honoring the god of forces or military might, would honor a god whom his fathers knew not. During the three and a half years of atheistic rule, a veiled female of the opera was installed as the "Goddess of Reason" by the French ruling body.

We come now to the last 6 verses of chapter 11. Verse 40 says, "and at the time of the end shall the king of the South push at him." Who is the "him"? Not the king of the North as we previously thought, but the subject of the previous four verses—France. It goes on to say, "...and the king of the North shall come against him like a whirlwind..." Who is the "him" the king of the North comes against like a whirlwind? Not the king of the South as we previously thought, but the subject of verses 36–39— France. Review again Uriah Smith's commentary on these verses. It does make sense.

Because in early Greek history, the kings of the North and South were involved in numerous battles, our minds go back to linking the king of the North in battle with the king of the South, at the time of the end. Because of this misconception we have cut off verses 40–45 from the continuance of the prophecy, and projected it into some distant unknown time in the future. This part of the prophecy is linked to verses 36–39, and the prophecy is already fulfilled in the past. Are we not doing a similarly foolish thing as the secret rapture people have done, e.g. cutting off the 70th week of the 70 week prophecy, and projecting it some 2000 years beyond the end of the 69th week?

Why are we cutting off the last six verses of Dan. 11 and projecting it way into the future, we know not when?

Let us examine verse 40 again, and, with Uriah Smith's help, see how accurately the prophecy has been fulfilled.

The time of the end began in 1798 at the demise of the Papacy. Verse 40 says,"…at the time of the end shall the king of the South push at him." The "him" of this sentence is not the king of the North, but the subject of the previous verses, France.

France had all but conquered Europe. England was yet to be subdued. In the early part of 1798 the French directory desired Napoleon to attack England. Napoleon thought that the attack on England would be better done in the autumn of the year. He persuaded the directory to allow him to attack Egypt to intercept Britain's Eastern trade.

Napoleon assembled a sizable fleet and a large army which landed and took Alexandria on July 2, 1798. On July 21, the Battle of the Pyramids was fought in which the relatively untrained Egyptian forces were no match for the disciplined French troops. The king of the South shall push at him—a minor resistance. Napoleon then made his way to Cairo entering the city on July 25, 1798.

Egypt was then in the control of France. The British fleet under Nelson then destroyed the French fleet. Turkey, the country then occupying the region of the North, considered Egypt a semi-dependency of the Ottoman Empire. Turkey came through Palestine to engage Napoleon driving him back to Egypt. Turkey inflicted on him his first retreat in battle. Turkish, British and Russian ships were involved in the encounter thus constituting the "many ships" stated in the prophecy.

"He shall enter also into the glorious land." It was through Palestine that the Turks defeated Napoleon. Edom, Moab and Ammon shall escape. The countries East of the Jordan. were spared by the king of the North (Turkey). "He shall stretch forth his hand ... and the land of Egypt shall not escape." Egypt was again in the control of the Ottoman Empire. Napoleon was then recalled to France by the French government.

Verse 44 says, "but tidings out of the east and out of the North shall trouble him; therefore he shall go forth with great fury to destroy, and to utterly make away many." Adam Clarke, a student of prophecy not of our faith, predicted in 1825 on the basis of this verse that there would be a war between Turkey (the king of the North) with Russia to the North and Persia to the East. A few years thereafter the Crimean war broke out in which Turkey declared war on Russia to its North and Persia to the East.

Then the last verse of the chapter reads, "and he shall plant the tabernacles of his palace between the seas in the glorious holy mountain..." The tabernacles (or the religion) of his palace (of the rulers of the king of the North—that is Islam) will be found planted between the seas (between the Mediterranean and the Dead seas) in the glorious holy mountain (in Jerusalem). It is there that we find the Dome of the Rock, the Mosque of Omar, the third most holy place of Islam right where Solomon's temple was supposed to have been located.

The rest of the verse says of the king of the North, "...yet he shall come to his end and none shall help him." When God proph-esied against Babylon, he said it will not be rebuilt, and it never has been rebuilt. The same was said of Tyre, and the site of the old city of Tyre is still not rebuilt. When God spoke of the end of the king of the North, he spoke nothing of utter devastation such as with Babylon or Tyre. He simply said that when the king of the North (the Ottoman Empire) comes to its end and none would help him. It is amazing how accurately this has been fulfilled as recorded by Uriah Smith in his comments on the Ottoman Empire in chapter 9 of *Thoughts on Revelation*. Uriah Smith does not link Dan. 11:45 with Rev. 9, but the connection is obvious.

The Ottoman empire began at the end of the five month prophetic period of Rev. 9. It was to last for "an hour and a day, and a month and a year"—or for 391 years and 15 days.

Josiah Litch in 1838 predicted, on the basis of this latter time prophecy that the Ottoman Empire would come to its end in Aug of 1840. Just before the fulfillment of the prophecy he predicted on the basis of his calculations of the hour, day, month and year prophecy that Turkey (the Ottoman Empire) would come to its end on August 11, 1840. On that very day the Ottoman Empire signed the agreement relinquishing its power to the control of the four great Christian powers of the West. Turkey (the Ottoman Empire) came to its end and its former allies were the ones to whom it relinquished its power. None did help him.

We now see the natural fulfillment of the prophecy as a sequence. A danger in looking for a last day battle between a king of the South and a king of the North is that we may be looking for this as a signpost in events during the time of the end. We may be looking for an event that has already occurred. We need to be ready regardless of interpretations of prophetic verses of the Bible, one way or the other. If we wait for a king of the north to come to his end before we make ready for Jesus' return, we may be playing desperately close to the close of probation.

SECTION 9

DANIEL 12

There should be no separation between Dan. 11 and Dan. 12. The angel continues instruction to Daniel. He starts with, "And at that time shall Michael stand up..." The question is raised, at what time? Some say, when the king of the North comes to his end and none shall help him.

When Michael "stands up," He takes the kingdom from the hands of His Father to rule. Probation is closed. If the interpretation of the last six verses of Dan. 11 is correct, and if "at that time" refers to when the king of the North comes to his end and none shall help him, then probation is already closed. The reasoning is that Michael stands up (close of probation) when the king of the North comes to his end.

Dan. 11:35 speaks of the time of the end—a time appointed. The angel describes events occurring during the time of the end which includes the last six verses of the chapter. When the angel says, "and at that time shall Michael stand up..." he is referring to the close of probation occurring <u>sometime after these mentioned events</u>. The time frame of "the time of the end," is not referring specifically to when the king of the North comes to his end. It should be pointed out that the Ottoman Empire came to its end in Aug 11, 840 but the Turkish nation in its weakened form continues on.

The rest of verse one is easily understood. It speaks of a time of trouble such as never was since there was a nation even to that same time. This appears to be national and international trouble, and should not be confused, as is so often done, with the great tribulation of the church mentioned in Matt. 24:21. "Immediately after the tribulation of those days shall the sun be darkened, and the moon shall not give her light, and the stars shall fall from heaven..." After the 1260 years of tribulation of the church, these signs appeared. Ellen White makes note of the fact that the persecution abated some years before the end of the 1260 years of Papal supremacy. That goes along with Matt. 24:22 "and except those days should be shortened, there should no flesh be saved." It should be clear that the signs mentioned occurred after the tribulation of those days and are distinct events separate from the great time of trouble at the end.

Dan. 12:2 touches on the special resurrection. In John 5:28, 29 Jesus speaks of two resurrections. "Marvel not at this: for the hour is coming, in which all that are in the graves shall hear His voice, and shall come forth; they that have done good, unto the resurrection of life; and they that have done evil, unto the resurrection of damnation."

In Rev. 20, these two resurrections are separated by 1000 years. The resurrection of the righteous occurs at the beginning of the 1000 years; the resurrection of the unrighteous occurs at the end of the 1000 years.

In Dan. 12:2 we have a resurrection where not all but "...many of them that sleep in the dust of the earth shall awake some to everlasting life, and some to shame and everlasting contempt." Here we have a partial resurrection involving some righteous, and some wicked.

Jesus told the high priest that hereafter he will "...see the Son of Man sitting on the right hand of power and coming in the clouds of heaven." Matt. 26:64. Apparently some of the wicked who were involved in Jesus' condemnation and crucifixion will be resurrected to behold His coming in glory. Ellen White states that all who die in the faith of the third angel's message will come forth to see Jesus at His coming. Verse four mentions that the book would be shut up and sealed even to the time of the end. It will not be understood or at least not clearly understood until the time of the end.

The latter part of verse four has been commented on. Some think it refers to increased knowledge of the word, and particularly the prophetic word. That has to be only a partial truth. None can deny the fabulous increase in knowledge in all fields of human endeavor. Knowledge shall be increased, and indeed it has been. Many shall run to and fro. For Daniel to predict this some 600 years BC is remarkable indeed! How could he have seen the rapid means of transportation we know today? Travel a little over 100 years ago was still primitive and not far removed from travel in Daniel's day.

We go to a question raised in Dan. 12:6. "How long shall it be to the end of these wonders?" Again that "how long" question is associated with the days of persecution. The answer is given in verse seven, "... it shall be for a time, times, and a half."

Here we see how God sometimes communicates His will. In the early part of Dan. 12, God speaks of end time events. Suddenly our attention is turned back to 538–1798. We need to point out these are so called "flash backs," seen so often in the books of Daniel and The Revelation. It is a fool hardy thing for anyone to decipher the book of Daniel or The Revelation as a continuous sequence. Utter confusion would result.

Verse 11 introduces a new time prophecy—the 1290-day prophecy. It states that "...from the time that the daily sacrifice (the continuance of desolation—Pagan Rome) shall be taken away and the abomination that maketh desolate (Papal Rome) set up," shall be 1290 days. This prophecy began in 508 when Clovis started the process which finally gave the Papacy its dominance in 538—the beginning of the 1260 year prophecy. From the year 508 AD to the year 1798 AD is 1290 years.

Verse 12 introduces still another time prophecy. A blessing is pronounced upon those who come to the 1335 days.

Beginning at 508, and adding 1335 brings us to the date 1843, the year before the great disappointment, and the beginning of the investigative judgment.

The book ends with the angel telling Daniel that he will rest, be asleep in death, and will stand in his lot at the end of the days. In other words, Daniel's name will come up for review in the investigative judgment at the end of the prophetic days as will all other professed followers of our Lord.

May that review be favorable to all of us who look forward to that great and blessed event—the coming of our Lord. Amen.

Revelation's Secrets Revealed

FOREWORD

Before looking into these concepts of Revelation, we must keep in mind that Revelation cannot be read as a continuous sequence. Revelation must be recognized as a prophecy with three repeat sequences of the true church, the apostate church and God's judgments on the apostate church.

The first sequence is the seven churches, the seven seals and the seven trumpets. The second sequence is Rev. 12 (the true church), Rev. 13 (the apostate church) and Rev. 16 (God's judgments on the apostate church). The third and last sequence omits the true church. It deals with Rev. 17 (the apostate church) and Rev. 18 (God's judgments upon the apostate church) which continues in the latter half of chapter 19 and all of chapter 20.

Another caution needs to be pointed out. John has a way of writing which can be easily misunderstood. He uses the phrase "...and after this..." which some have interpreted to mean what follows is in sequence to what immediately preceded it. Quite often what follows is an unrelated vision to that which preceded it.

The book of Revelation is a Revelation of Jesus Christ. It is a prophecy of what would take place in the Christian church from the time Jesus established it all the way down to His second coming. To us today, most of the book is now history. Very little is left to be fulfilled before the second coming.

I make no apologies for referring to the work of Uriah Smith in his book, *The Prophecies of Daniel and The Revelation*. I find it a very rational approach to the prophecy, and it is endorsed by the Lord's servant Ellen White in the book *Evangelism*. What better endorsement can you want than that of the Lord's servant!

With these remarks in mind, let us now look at this very exciting book. —The Prophecies of the Book of Revelation.

SECTION 1

FORMAT OF THE BOOK OF REVELATION

The book of Revelation has three repeat sequences instead of four as we have in Daniel. In Daniel the last two repeat sequences omit Babylon. In the last repeat of Revelation, the true church is omitted.

Each of Revelation's three sequences covers three topics. These are (a) the true church (b) the apostate church (c) God's judgments on the apostate church.

The above three topics, (a), (b) and (c) are repeated three times in the prophecy. The true church is omitted in the third repeat.

We may diagram the sequences as follows:

The True Church	The Apostate Church	God's Judgment on the Apostasy
1. The seven churches	The seven seals	The seven trumpets
2. The woman clothed with the sun. Rev. 12	The leopard-like beast. Rev. 13	The plague chapter Rev. 16
3. True church omitted	The harlot woman and her daugters	God's judgments on Babylon. Rev. 18
		The Battle of Armageddon
		Final destruction of The wicked

There are sanctuary images given before the seven churches, the seven seals and the seven trumpets. Between the sixth and seventh seals, the sealing work of Rev. 7 is given. The seventh seal covers the second coming of our Lord.

Rev. 8:2–5 are sanctuary images preceding the sounding of the seven trumpets. Chapters 8:6–9:21 pictures events occurring during the sounding of six trumpets. Rev. 10–11:14 depicts scenes on earth occurring before the sounding of the seventh trumpet. The seventh trumpet is sounded in Rev. 11:15. Probation is closed and end time events occur rapidly.

Rev. 12 repeats the history of the true church. It deals entirely with the church from the birth of Jesus to the end time.

Rev. 13 is the second repeat of the apostasy. In the seals, the apostasy deals entirely with the mother church. In Rev. 13, the apostasy includes the harlot daughter churches, leopard beast and two-horned, lamb-like beast.

Rev. 13 introduces the mark of the beast. Rev. 14, appropriately placed, gives the stern warning to those who worship the beast and receives his mark.

Rev. 16 is the second repeat of God's judgments on apostate Christianity.

There is no mention of the true church in the third repeat in the series.

Rev. 17 pictures apostate Christianity as a harlot woman who gave birth to harlot daughter churches.

Rev. 18 is the third repeat of God's judgment on the apostasy—God's judgments on Babylon.

The latter half of Rev. 19 is the Bible's description of Armageddon. In my view there is a millennial interlude in the Battle of Armageddon allowing the universe to examine the evidence for the final destruction of the wicked which is pictured in Rev. 20.

Rev. 21 and 22 give us only a partial view of the glories awaiting those who choose to accept the very generous provisions offered to a sinful world.

Now let us examine this exciting book—"The Revelation of Jesus Christ, which God gave unto him to show unto His servants things which must shortly come to pass."

SECTION 2

REVELATION CHAPTER 1

Let us start by observing a few points of interest in Rev., chapter 1. God speaking through his servant John says in verse one, "...to show unto His servants things which must shortly come to pass." In verse three we have the words "...for the time is at hand." In God's timetable, the time between the writing of the book of Rev., AD 96, and the second coming of Jesus, is considered but a short span.

In Rev. 1:5, Jesus is the "faithful witness and the first begotten of the dead." This verse is a key to understanding Psa. 2:7, "... Thou art my Son; this day have I begotten thee." John 3:16 speaks of Jesus as the "...only begotten Son..." John 1:14, "...the only begotten of the Father." John 1:18, "... the only begotten Son, which is in the bosom of the Father..." 1 John 4:9, "God sent His only begotten Son into the world..." and Heb. 1:5 quotes Psalms 2:7, "... this day have I begotten thee."

Rev. 1:5 clarifies "begotten" as not related to physical birth, but Jesus coming from the dead. This is reinforced by Col. 1:15 and 18 where it says that Jesus is the "... firstborn of every creature... the firstborn from the dead." Acts 26:23 says, "That Christ should suffer and that He should be the first that should rise from the dead." Paul, in Acts 13:30, says that God raised Jesus from the dead.

In Acts 13:33 Paul says, "God hath fulfilled the same unto us their children, in that He hath raised up Jesus again; as it is also written in the second Psalm, Thou art my Son, this day have I begotten thee."

Jesus is spoken of as the firstborn of the dead. Moses died and was resurrected. The real meaning of Jesus being the <u>first begotten from the dead</u>, is that by virtue of His resurrection, we may have eternal life. Not first in time, but first in importance. No resurrection could occur without Christ being risen from the dead.

Rev. 1:6 is exciting! We are made "kings and priests unto God and His Father." Rev. 5:10 reinforces that with, "and hast made us unto our God, kings and priests." To the Laodicean church he writes in Rev. 3:21, "To him that overcometh will I grant to sit with me in My throne, even as I also overcame, and am set down with My Father in His throne." What are we doing sitting in God's throne? We are made kings, sitting with Jesus in His throne. Paul in Rom. 8:17 says, "and if children, then heirs; heirs of God, and joint-heirs with Christ." Ellen White says we do not fully understand what is meant by being partakers of the divine nature.

Rev. 1:7 where, "…every eye shall see Him, and they also which pierced Him," when placed together with Dan. 12:2, "and <u>many</u> of them that sleep in the dust of the earth shall awake, <u>some</u> to everlasting life, and <u>some</u> to shame and everlasting contempt," support the concept of a partial resurrection to take place prior to the general resurrection at Christ second coming. Ellen White states also that all who die in the faith of the three angel's messages will come forth to see Jesus second coming. In the partial resurrection <u>some</u> come up to everlasting life, and <u>some</u> to shame and everlasting contempt. In the general resurrection the righteous are raised at the beginning of the millennium and the wicked at the end of the millennium.

Rev. 1:10 is the frequently misused text quoted to sustain Sunday observance as the Christian Sabbath. Which day is the Lord's day? Ex. 20:10, "but the <u>seventh day</u> is the <u>Sabbath of the Lord</u> thy God." Eze. 20:12, "Moreover I gave them <u>My</u>

Sabbaths…" Eze. 20:20, "and hallow My Sabbath…." Which day does Jesus claim as His? God was not speaking of Sunday observance in the Old Testament. Isa. 58:13, "… from doing thy pleasure on My holy day;" We should not use Rev. 1:10, "I was in the spirit on the Lord's day…" in a contextual fashion ending up teaching error based on a limited view of one verse.

John saw Jesus walking in the midst of seven golden candlesticks (Verse 13). Seven individual lamp stands, not the single seven-branched candlestick (singular) of the holy place. John describes Jesus in his glorified state. The description matches that given in Dan. 10. Jesus had in His right hand seven stars. A sharp two edged sword proceeded from His mouth. Rev. 19:15 pictures Jesus also with a sharp sword proceeding from His mouth. "The word of God is quick and powerful and sharper than any two-edged sword…" Heb. 4:12. Rev. 19 says he will smite the nations with the sword of His mouth. He will destroy them by His word.

Then Jesus tells John what the seven stars in His right hand represent. They are the angels or leaders of the seven churches and the seven candlesticks are the seven churches.

SECTION 3

REVELATION CHAPTERS 2 & 3

Rev. 1 is a prologue of sanctuary images preceding the messages to the churches given in chapters 2 & 3.

What evidences do we have that the messages to the churches are messages to the Christian churches during the entire Christian dispensation? We will notice that the message to the first church, Ephesus, is the only message that mentions "apostles." Rev. 2:2 "...thou hast tried them which say, they are apostles, and are not, and hast found them liars." The church's name of Ephesus means, "first or desirable." The middle church, Thyatira, running from 538 to 1798 AD parallels the three and a half years of drought during the reign of Ahab and his wife Jezebel (figurative Jezebel) "...which calleth herself a prophetess, to teach and to seduce my servants to commit fornication..." The last church, Laodicea, means judging the people, and indeed we are living in the last days, the days of the investigative judgment.

All of the churches are addressed with the opening statement. Unto the <u>angel</u> of the church of _____. Is God speaking to a literal unfallen angel who is directing the affairs of the churches? No. Speaking to the <u>angel</u> (the leadership) of the church of Ephesus, He says,"...because thou hast left thy first love. Remember therefore from whence thou are fallen, and repent..." Angels do not leave their first love. Angels have no need to repent.

The reprimand to the angel (leadership) of the church of Pergamos reads, "… because thou hast there them that hold the doctrine of Balaam, who taught Balac to cast a stumbling block before the children of Israel, to eat things sacrificed unto idols, and to commit fornication."

To the angel in Thyatira, Jesus reprimands them for sufferings that woman Jezebel (not literal Jezebel) to seduce His servants to commit fornication and to eat things sacrificed unto idols.

To the angel of the church of Sardis, Jesus said, "…I have not found thy works perfect before God." Repent.

To the angel of the church of Laodecia, Jesus has some pointed and scathing rebukes. They are neither cold nor hot—neither enthusiastic and aflame nor dead with inactivity. They are wretched, miserable, and poor and blind and naked. Counsel is given to change this state of affairs.

The messages are for the churches but they are addressed to the angels of—or the leadership of the churches. God knows that as the leadership goes, so go the churches.

In Rev. 1:20 Jesus had in His hand seven stars which he states are the angels (or the leadership) of the seven churches.

It was pointed out in comments on Daniel 8, that the little horn—Rome—would cast some of the host—God's people—and of the stars—the leadership—to the ground and stamp upon them. In Jesus hand were held the seven stars; the angels of the seven churches; the leadership of the seven churches—is here indicated.

To each of the seven churches, the encouragement is given; "to him that overcometh…" Various incentives are held out to those willing to overcome.

Another repeated statement to the churches reads, "I know they works…" Is God concerned about works? James 2:17 says, "even so, faith if it hath not works, is dead, being alone." James goes on to say, in verse 20, "but wilt thou know O vain man, that faith without works is dead?" In other words faith if not accompanied by performance is not a saving faith at all.

So the messages to the churches are couched in the framework of works—"I know thy works…" Is Jesus concerned about salvation? He is supremely concerned about salvation which is not by works. However, Jesus says, "…I know thy works…he that overcometh…" and there follows the stated reward for overcoming. In Rev. 22:12 Jesus says, "and behold I come quickly; and my reward is with me, to give every man according as his works shall be." Is this "reward" eternal life? Eternal life is a gift of which we all receive the same amount. But rewards are given according as our works shall be.

Another recurrent statement at the end of each message to the churches is, "He that hath an ear, let him hear what the Spirit saith unto the churches." The messages are directed not only to the seven churches (plural) in Asia minor but to all churches in the Christian era (Ephesus to Laodecia).

Attention should be called to the symbolism used in the messages to the churches. In the message to Smyrna we read, "…I know the blasphemy of them which say, they are Jews and are not, but are the synagogue of Satan." Here "Jews" is used as given in Rom. 2:28, 29. "For he is not a Jew which is one outwardly; neither is that circumcision which is outward in the flesh, but he is a Jew which is one inwardly; and circumcision is that of the heart, in the spirit and not in the letter whose praise is not of men, but of God." We see the same use of the term "Jews" in the Philadelphia message (Rev. 3:9).

To the church of Pergamos, "…thou hast there them that hold the doctrine Baalam who taught Balac to cast a stumbling block before the children of Israel…" Here, the work of Balaam is used as an example of what was going on in the church of Pergamos.

Jezebel, who was destroyed years before, is mentioned in Thyatira as teaching Paganism in the time of this church. The suggestion of the Protestant Reformation is seen in Rev. 2:23 where the Lord said, "…and I will kill her children with death…"

This harmonizes with Rev. 17:5 where the harlot mother church has daughter churches which are also harlots. The harlot daughter churches are Protestant churches that cling to Old Catholic doctrines having no basis in the Word of God.

Two other points of interest may be mentioned. First, in the message to the Pergamos church we have this statement, "…even in those days wherein <u>Antipas</u> was my faithful martyr…" This church is dated around 323 to 538 AD This was when the Papacy was developing after the demise of the Roman Empire. The term "Antipas," some suggest, may refer to as <u>Anti-Papacy</u>. Those who were anti-Papacy were Jesus faithful martyrs.

The second point of interest is seen in the encouragement to the Laodecians to overcome. The reward for overcoming is that we will sit with Jesus in His throne even as He overcame and was set down with His Father in His throne. What are we doing sitting with Jesus in His throne? Paul says in Rom. 8:17, "and if children, then heirs; heirs of God, joint-heirs with Christ…" If heirs we inherit all things with Jesus who inherits all things from His Father. We are made <u>kings</u> and priests unto God. Rev. 1:6 and Rev. 5:10.

Detailed comments on the specific messages to the churches can be found in the excellent commentaries on these verses by Uriah Smith in *The Prophecies of Daniel and The Revelation.*

SECTION 4

REVELATION CHAPTERS 4 & 5

Chapter four begins with the sentence, "after this I looked..." This must not be understood as events following the Laodecian church. John is describing events in heaven leading up to the opening of the seven seals. The seven seals take us back to the history of the apostasy—that which developed the "man of sin"—the Papacy (2 Thess. 2:3).

After the vision of the seven churches, John sees another vision. He sees a throne in heaven with one sitting on it. He briefly describes the One seated on the throne in verse three as appearing "...like a jasper and a sardine stone." Who is the One seated on the throne? Rev. 4:11 suggests Jesus as the One seated on the throne because He created all things. However, Rev. 5 pictures the One seated on the throne as God the Father. The lamb appears and takes the book out of the hand of the One seated on the throne. Therefore the One on the throne is God the Father from whose hands the lamb (Jesus) takes the book and opens the seals thereof. John sees around the throne 24 seats upon which sat 24 elders. Who are these elders and where did they come from? In Rev. 5:8, 9 these elders sing of their experience. "...for thou wast slain and hast <u>redeemed us</u> to God, by thy blood, out of every kindred, and tongue, and people, and nation." As Uriah Smith suggests, these are not people seen at the close of time. Their song begins with "...thou are worthy to take the book, and to open the seals thereof." They sing this song before the seals were opened. The seals are a prophecy of the apostasy which would develop—coming out of the true church.

Where did they come from? Their song tells us that they were "redeemed... by thy blood." They came from this earth. They were in heaven before the seals were opened. Isaiah speaks prophetically in Isa. 26:19, "thy dead men shall live, together with my dead body shall they arise..." Matt. 27:52, 53 gives us the fulfillment of this prophecy. "And the graves were opened and many bodies of the saints which slept arose, and came out of the graves after His resurrection and went into the holy city and appeared unto many." Eph. 4:8 adds this, "Wherefore he saith, when he ascended up on high, he led captivity captive and gave gifts unto men."

John tells us that "...there were seven lamps of fire burning before the throne, which are the seven spirits of God." This is a symbolic way of saying the Holy Spirit was present.

He sees four beasts, or living creature in and around the throne. Who are these living creatures? Rev. 5:8, 9 gives us some insight into who the living creatures may be. "And when he had taken the book, the four beasts (living creatures) and four and twenty elders fell down before the Lamb, having every one of them harps, and golden vials full of odours, which are the prayers of saints. And they sung a new song, saying, Thou are worthy to take the book, and to open the seals thereof: for thou wast slain, and hast redeemed us to God by thy blood out of every kindred, and tongue, and people, and nation."

Two points should be noted in these verses.

1 - The four beasts (living creatures) and the 24 elders, both had "...golden vials, full of odours, which are the prayers of the saints." Both of these are functioning as priests. We recall Rev. 1:6 and Rev. 5:10 where the redeemed are made kings and priests unto God.

2 - Both groups sing the song, "...for thou wast slain and hast redeemed us to God..." Apparently if we take these verses at face value, the living creatures are also people redeemed from this earth. These living creatures were also seen by Ezekiel. See (Eze. 1:5,6,10). Ezekiel described them as cherubims. (See Eze.

10:20). We may say, that if these four living creatures are cherubims then they could not be redeemed from the earth. The redeemed will sit with Jesus in His throne. This is as close a relationship to God as one can get. None can know, but is it possible that some select redeemed could be given the role of cherubims around God's throne?

Chapter five is a continuation of the sanctuary images preceding the opening of the seals and should not be conceptually separated from chapter four.

The One seated on the throne held a book, "…written within and on the backside, sealed with seven seals." A voice raised the question as to who was worthy to open the book, and to loose the seals thereof."

None was found in heaven, or in earth, neither under the earth that was able to open the book. Neither to look thereon.

John "wept much" because of this dilemma. One of the elders comforted John, saying that Jesus "…had prevailed to open the book and to loose the seals." In other words, only Jesus could open the book with the seven seals which contained the history of the apostasy.

John sees Jesus represented as a Lamb slain, in the midst of the throne, the four beasts, and the 24 elders. The slain Lamb had seven eyes, which are the seven spirits of God sent forth into all the earth. The eyes of the Lamb represent the Holy Spirit, illustrating the close fellowship and cooperation of Jesus and the Holy Spirit in working for the lost "…in all the earth."

When the Lamb (Jesus) came and took the book out of the right hand of Him that sat upon the throne, the four beasts (living creatures), together with the 24 elders, fell down before the Lamb (Jesus) and sung the new song, "thou are worthy to take the book, and to open the seals thereof: for thou wast slain, and hast redeemed us to God by thy blood out of every kindred, and tongue, and people, and nation. And hast made us unto our God kings and priests; and we shall reign on the earth."

Here, not only the elders, but also the four beasts (living creatures) sing that Jesus has "…made us unto our God kings and priests."

Verses 11 and 12 depict a mighty chorus shouting or perhaps singing with a loud voice that magnificent chorus of praise, "Worthy is the Lamb that was slain to receive power, and riches, and wisdom, and strength, and honour, and glory, and blessing."

And what an echo follows in verse 13! The entire universe reverberates with that hymn of praise! "And every creature which is in heaven and on the earth, and under the earth, and such as are in the sea, and all that are in them, heard I saying, blessing, and honour, and glory, and power, be unto Him that sitteth upon the throne, (God the Father) and unto the Lamb (Jesus) forever and ever."

This magnificent scene occurred before the opening of the seals. How did all creatures in heaven, on earth, under the earth and such as are in the sea join this chorus of praise? Revelation is a book of symbols. Jesus, the Lamb was slain, thus ratifying and confirming the plan of salvation. The angels, the four living creatures, and the 24 elders verbalize the confirmation of the plan, "worthy is the Lamb…" to receive power, riches, wisdom, strength, honor, glory and blessing. The rest of the universe, every living creature in heaven, earth, under the earth and in the sea is in perfect harmony with the plan and symbolically glorified God on His throne and the Lamb who made salvation and the cleansing of the universe possible.

SECTION 5

REVELATION CHAPTER 6

Chapter 6 is a brief progressive prophecy of the development of apostasy coming out of the true church. In 2 Thess 2:3,4,7 Paul speaks of a "...man of sin...who opposeth and exalted himself above all that is called God, or that is worshipped; so that he as God sitteth in the temple of God, shewing himself that he is God... for the mystery of iniquity doth already work."

In Paul's day the departure from the true faith had already begun. That which would produce the "man of sin" (the Papal system) was already at work.

When the first seal was opened, John was invited to come and see. He saw a white horse. The rider had a bow in hand. He had a crown given him, and he went forth conquering and to conquer. The original church in apostolic times is here described. It was pure as depicted by the white horse. Its achievements against great odds is depicted as "conquering and to conquer."

But we recall Jesus' reprimand to the Ephesus church, "thou hast left thy first love." As time went on, and the promised return of Jesus seemed delayed and in the distant future; zeal and enthusiasm waned.

The second seal was broken. Another horse was seen—this horse was red. The church had lost its purity. False teachings were brought into the church. The rider was given power to take peace from the earth, and that they should kill one another. We are given here a picture of fighting and disunity in the church, which would divide the church into God's true followers (pictured in the seven churches) and the mystery of iniquity which would develop into the Papal system.

When the third seal was opened, John sees a black horse. This period of the apostate church begins when Constantine the Great joins its ranks. The black horse depicts the depths of degradation to which the apostate church had fallen. Commercialism in the church was depicted by the rider having a pair of balances in his hand, and a voice calling out "...a measure of wheat for a penny; and three measures of barley for a penny."

The fourth seal was opened, and John sees a pale horse. Death was the name of the rider and hell—or the grave followed with him. This horse represents the work of the apostate church during the 1260 years of papal supremacy. The pale horse with death as its rider was an ominous prophecy for the followers of the true church. It states that, "...power was given unto them over the fourth part of the earth, to kill with the sword, and with hunger, and with death, and with the beast of the earth." This fitly describes the work of the papacy during the 1260 years of its dominance. Who is represented by the "fourth part of the earth?" In Rev. 16:13, the world of the unsaved is divided into three parts, 1) dragon-pagan religions 2) beast-the papal system 3) the false prophet-the apostate protestant churches. The fourth part refers to God's true church, which would be persecuted by the papal system during the dark ages.

The fourth seal ended, or takes us to the time of the early protestant reformers. Speaking of the "great tribulation" to come to God's true church during the time of papal supremacy, Jesus said that "...except those days should be shortened, there should no flesh be saved." Jesus is saying that if the 1260 days of persecution were not shortened there would be nothing left of the true church. From the time of Martin Luther and other early reformers, there was increasing erosion of the papal power to persecute. Ellen White states that persecution had abated years before the "deadly wound" was inflicted in 1798. It should be emphasized again that the tribulation referred to by Jesus in Matt. 24:21 is not to be confused with the time of trouble, "...such as never was since there was a nation even to that same time..." mentioned in Dan. 12:1. The tribulation of Matt. 24:21 is the tribulation of the church, 538–1798 AD This is confirmed by Matt. 24:29 where "Immediately after the tribulation of those days..." the sun was darkened, the moon was obscured, and the stars did fall from heaven. The time of trouble mentioned in Dan. 12:1 is a time of trouble among the nations of earth, after probation is closed.

When the fifth seal was opened, persecution had abated. The power of the Roman church was curtailed by the rising protestant reformation. The end had not yet come. The martyred saints are figuratively crying out for God to avenge their blood on those who dwelt upon the earth. They are told that they should rest for a season longer until their fellow servants and their brethren should be killed as they were.

The sixth seal opens with a huge earthquake—the Lisbon earthquake of Nov 1, 1755. This earthquake was so massive that it was felt in Europe, Africa and the Americas. Following the earthquake, the sun was darkened on May 19, 1780; the moon became as blood May 19, 1780, the great meteoric shower of stars occurred Nov 13, 1833. We should notice that Matt. 24 says, these signs would occur "...immediately after the tribulation of those days." The sign in the sun and moon occurred before the end of the 1260 days. It occurred however, after the tribulation ceased. In Rev. 6:12, 13, the signs in the sun moon and stars would occur after the great earthquake of Nov 1, 1755, and so they did—May 19, 1780 and Nov 13, 1833. The prophecy then skips to the end of time. Rev. 6:14 describes "...the heaven departed as a scroll when it is rolled together; and every mountain and island were moved out of their places."

The remaining three verses (verses 15–17) describe the terror of the lost.

There is nothing mentioned about the apostate church when the fifth and sixth seals are opened. Rising Protestantism during the fifth seal curbed the activities of the papal church finally ending in the "deadly wound" of 1798. Details of the apostasy starting during the Protestant Reformation—fifth seal—and papal aberrations following the healing of the "deadly wound" are given in detail in the second and third sequences of this great book—The Revelation of Jesus Christ.

SECTION 6

REVELATION CHAPTER 7

Inserted between events of the sixth and seventh seals is the chapter on the sealing work and the 144,000. Rev. 7.

Again we see John starting this chapter with, "and after these things I saw..." this is not to be understood as the events of chapter seven follow the events of chapters six. John is simply saying, after the vision of chapter six, I saw another vision. Chapter six ends with "...the heaven's departed as a scroll" etc. the second coming. The events described in chapter seven certainly occur before Jesus appears in the clouds of heaven, where the servants of God are sealed in their foreheads.

Four angels were seen holding the four winds of the earth. Strife and trouble in the world such as never was since there was a nation (Dan. 12:1) would be held till the servants of God are sealed in their foreheads.

The number sealed in their foreheads was given as 144,000. Twelve thousand are sealed from each tribe. The tribes are named. Dan is omitted because of idolatry (see Judges 18). Manassas replaces Dan in the Rev. 7 list.

Are the tribes mentioned here literal descendents from Abraham? No! It is inconceivable that 12000 literal Jews from each of the twelve tribes could be found today to provide a literal fulfillment of the prophecy. Furthermore Jesus rejected the Jewish nation as his representatives when he declared in Matt. 23:38, "Behold your house is left unto you desolate." We must conclude therefore that the tribes mentioned composing the

144,000 are spiritual Jews as mentioned by Paul in Gal. 3:29, "and if ye be Christ's then are ye Abraham's seed, and heirs according to the promise."

The next question arises. Is the number literal or symbolic? One may say, if the tribal names are symbolic, why would the number be literal? There is no clear cut answer to this question as I know it in either Rev. 7 or the Spirit of Prophecy writing. The question has been raised time and again as to who are the 144,000.

It should be pointed out that people have been sealed for eternal life before the sealing of Rev. 7. See 2 Cor. 1:22 where God "who hath also sealed us and given the earnest of the spirit in our hearts." Also see Eph. 1:13, "...in whom also after that ye believed, ye were sealed with that Holy Spirit of promise." And Eph. 4:30, "and grieve not the Holy Spirit of God, whereby ye are sealed unto the day of redemption."

Ellen White gives some insight as to who the 144,000 are. In SDA Bible Commentary Vol. 7, Pg 977, she writes, "Sunday keeping is not yet the mark of the beast and will not be until the decree goes forth causing men to worship this idol Sabbath. The time will come when this day will be the test but that time has not come yet" (From MS 118, 1899).

She further writes, "The Lord has shown me clearly that the image of the beast will be formed before probation closes, for it is to be the great test for the people of God, by which their eternal destiny will be decided" (Rev. 13:11–17 Quoted ibid 976).

She goes on to say, "This is the test that the people of God must have before they are sealed. All who prove their loyalty to God by observing His law, and refusing to accept a spurious Sabbath, will rank under the banner of the Lord God Jehovah, and will receive the seal of the living God. Those who yield the truth of heavenly origin and accept the Sunday Sabbath, will receive the mark of the beast." (Letter 11, 1890) ibid 976.

Here we see Ellen White indicating there will be a special sealing at a special time, in the future, when the image of the beast is set up and the mark of the beast enforced. At that time, and apparently at that time only, those who are alive will choose God's Sabbath and receive the seal of the living God in their foreheads, and those accepting the false Sabbath, receive the mark of the beast.

Here we are faced with a special sealing at a special time when the mark of the beast is enforced. Do we have any Bible evidence of a special sealing at a special time in the future? The answer is yes. It is found in the sealing work of Rev. 7. Here we have a special sealing because it produces a special group—the 144,000. It occurs at a special time just before the close of human probation. The angels are told to hold the winds "...till we have sealed the servants of God in their foreheads." They will hold till God's servants are sealed then they will let the winds of strife do their work. We understand this as the great time of trouble which will come upon the earth when Michael stands—probation is closed (see Dan. 12:1).

A special sealing at a special time is mentioned by the Spirit of Prophecy writings. A special sealing at a special time is given in Rev. 7 and this sealing results in the 144,000.

It should be mentioned that the seal of God is placed only in the forehead—a voluntary mental assent to God's way. The mark of the beast is placed in the forehead of those who believe the false Sabbath. The mark is placed in the right hand of those who may not believe the enforced keeping of the false Sabbath, but who go along with the law of the land enforcing the observance of the idol Sabbath. We believe that the seal of the living God is the seventh-day Sabbath. Its voluntary acceptance is described as a seal placed in the forehead. This will be expanded upon in the discussion of Rev. 13. in conjunction with the mark of the beast.

Again at verse 9 is another "after this..." of author John. He sees a "great multitude" which no man could number. Some say, the 144,000 were numbered. This group was so large that "...no man could number." Is John seeing the 144,000? Or is he seeing all of the redeemed? In Rev. 7:4 John says, "...I heard the number of them which were sealed." Then in verse 9 he said, "and after this I beheld…" I heard; now I see. Is he seeing the 144,000? We notice that this group came from "all nations, and kindred, and peoples and tongues…" Similar language is seen in the three angels' messages where the gospel is to be preached to "…every nation, and kindred, and tongue, and people." Rev. 14:6. The language of the three angels' messages is directed to people of the end time – "every nation, kindred, tongue and people." The great multitude which John saw in Rev. 7:9 also came from every nation, kindred, tongue and people. Since the focus of Rev. 7 is the 144,000, it is very likely that the "great multitude" that John saw was the 144,000, but the group appeared so large that John simply says, "…no man could number" them. It was impossible, or impractical to count them. Rev. 7:14 lends support to this view. They "…came out of great tribulation" — the great time of trouble at the end when the mark of the beast was enforced. Rev. 7:16 also supports this concept. "They shall hunger no more, neither thirst any more; neither shall the sun light on them, nor any heat." These apparently passed through the great time if trouble and also the time of the seven last plagues, when the sun was given power to "…scorch men with fire."

Ellen White uses Rev. 7:9 in a slightly different setting. She speaks of those nearest to God's throne "…who were once zealous in the cause of Satan but who plucked as brands from the burning have followed their Saviour with deep intense devotion." *The Great Controversy* p. 665

"Next are those who perfected Christian characters in the midst of falsehood and infidelity, who honored the law of God when the Christian world declared it void." This group appears to be the 144,000 who perfected Christian characters during the "great test" when the image to the beast was set up and the mark of the beast enforced.

She says, "and beyond is the "great multitude, which no man could number of all nations, and kindreds, and people and tongues."

Her use of the statement, "great multitude, which no man could number of all nations and kindreds, and people and tongues" to apply to the entire host of the redeemed does not do violence to Rev. 7:9 being applied to the 144,000. After all the entire host of the redeemed also comes from every nation, kindred, tongues and people. (GC p665) Ellen White indicates that the 144,000 will be those translated without seeing death. They obviously would have passed "the great test" by which all who live at that time must be sealed.

SECTION 7

REVELATION CHAPTER 8

Rev. chapters 8:2 to chapter 11 is a prophetic unit.

In chapter 8, the first verse belongs with the discussion of the seals. When the seventh seal is opened, there is silence in heaven about the space of half and hour. A half hour in the day-for-a-year principle is about one week. Why will there be silence in heaven for about half an hour? Matt. 25:31 says, "when the Son of Man shall come in His glory, and all the holy angels with Him, then shall He sit upon the throne of His glory…" When heaven is emptied for that great event, then will there be silence in heaven for about the space of half an hour.

Ellen White confirms that we will journey to our heavenly home in the space of one week. Why one week? Certainly Jesus can get us there in a moment. Perhaps we will get our first view of the wonders of the created universe as we brush by galaxy after galaxy on our way to our heavenly home. Negotiating space between here and the New Jerusalem in one week, I can assure you, we would certainly be moving rapidly. We would be in motion in one week far faster than the speed of light.

Rev. 8:2–6 portrays sanctuary images that precede the sounding of the seven trumpets. Seven angels are seen with seven trumpets. Another angel stood by the altar. He had a golden censer. He was given much incense to be offered with the prayers of all saints. John sees the prayers of the saints arising with the smoke of the incense.

Then the angel took the censer and filled it with fire from the altar and cast it into the earth. Then there were "...voices and thunderings, and lightenings and an earthquake." This symbolic act of the angel tells us that probation is closed. No further prayers ascend to God in the sanctuary on high.

In Rev. 11:19, we have a similar statement. At the sounding of the seventh trumpet there would be lightenings, and voices, and thunderings, and an earthquake and great hail.

In Rev. 16:18, when the seventh angel pours out his vial upon the earth there were voices, and thunderings, and lightening, a great earthquake, and a great hail.

When the angel casts the censer to earth, probation is closed. When the seventh trumpet sounds probation is closed. When the seventh vial of plagues is poured out, probation is closed. The voice, lightenings, thunders, earthquake and great hail is the focal point of these three textual groups.

The seven trumpets are trumpets of war. They represent God's prophecy of the judgments to befall the apostate Christian church. Pagan Rome had been divided into the 10 kingdoms by the end of the fourth century. Christians were persecuted by pagan Rome from its very onset. Daniel predicted that pagan Rome would have "...indignation against the holy covenant." But it would have "...intelligence with them that forsake the holy covenant." (See Dan. 11:30). Apostasy began in Paul's day. Compromise with error developed gradually until apostate Christianity resembled paganism so closely that Constantine the Great could be designated a Christian. Constantine's death occurred in 337 AD History dates the decline and fall of the Roman Empire from the date of Constantine's death. By the end of the fourth century AD, the apostate church backed by its illicit connection with the arm of government, began to assume increasing political and spiritual control of almost all affairs of human activity. The trumpets of war (God's judgments on the apostate church) began at the end of the fourth century AD, and the successive trumpets follow ending with the close of probation. When the seventh trumpet sounds, "...the kingdoms of this world are become the kingdoms of our Lord and of His Christ." Probation is closed.

It should be pointed out that the seven trumpets (God's judgment on the apostate Christian church) has its parallel in the seven last plagues where God's judgments are poured out upon spiritual Babylon (harlot mother church and harlot daughter churches). Modern Babylon is modern Christian apostasy. It will be shown that the seven last plagues targets Babylon and is not a universal phenomena.

This close parallel of the trumpets with the seven last plagues can be seen by comparing each trumpet noted in Rev. 8–11 with a corresponding plague in Rev. 16.

We will find that the first trumpet sounds and hail fire and blood were cast upon the earth. In the plague chapter, the first vial is pored upon the earth. When the second trumpet sounds, a fiery mountain falls into the sea. The second angel poured out his vial into the sea. The third trumpet sounds, and a fiery star falls upon the rivers and fountains of water. The third angel pours his vial upon the rivers and fountains of waters. When the fourth trumpet sounds, the sun was smitten along with the moon and stars. When the fourth vial was poured out, the sun scorched men with heat. When the fifth trumpet sounds, the sun and the air were darkened by the smoke of the pit. The fifth vial caused darkness on the seat of the beast. The sixth trumpet caused the loosening of four angels controlling the river Euphrates. The sixth plague caused the drying up of the waters of the river Euphrates. When the seventh trumpet sounds, as when the seventh vial is poured out, there were voices, lightenings, thunderings, a great earthquake and hail. When the seventh trumpet sounds, probation is closed. When the seventh vial is poured out, probation is also closed.

We should be able to see the parallel here. These two lines of prophecy deal with God's judgment against an apostate church, the trumpets show God's chastisement of the apostate church before and during the dark ages. The seven last plagues are God's judgment on the last day apostate church (harlot mother church and harlot daughter churches).

Another point of interest is the target of these war-like trumpets. All of the trumpets, except the fifth and the seventh, target the "third part" of. The seventh trumpet involves the whole world, not just the "third part." What is meant by the trumpets targeting the "third part?" To understand this we turn to Rev. 16:13 where the three parts of the unsaved are mentioned. These are 1) dragon 2) beast 3) false prophet. The dragon here is in reference to the dragon power of Rev. 12:3, 4. "And there appeared another wonder in heaven; and behold a great red dragon, having seven heads and ten horns, and seven crowns upon his heads. And his tail drew the third part of the stars of heaven and did cast them to the earth; ...and the dragon stood before the woman which was ready to be delivered, for to devour her child as soon as it was born." The dragon here represents not only Satan and specifically Herod who sought the young child's life, but also pagan Rome the power under which Herod functioned. Thus the dragon in Rev. 16:13 represents all pagan or non-Christian religions of the world. The beast of Rev. 16:13 refers to the beast of Rev. 13:1–10 which symbolizes the papal system of Christianity. The false prophet is the same as the Lamb-like beast of Rev. 13:11–18 or apostate Protestantism. Thus we have the three divisions of the entire system of false religions (dragon—paganism or false non-Christian religions), beast (the Papacy—Catholicism) and the false prophet (apostate or fallen Protestantism).

If we examine the times covered by the seven trumpets, we find the first trumpet covering a military event starting around 395 AD. At this time the target could not be the dragon power, (pagan Rome) for empire Rome was now divided into the 10 kingdoms. Neither could it be the false prophet (apostate Protestantism), for Protestantism never got started until the sixth trumpet. The only conclusion left is the "third part" mentioned in trumpets one to four and six must be the papal system which alone existed at the time. The target of trumpet five must automatically be considered to involve the "third part" (the papal system), since all others but the seventh targets the "third part." The seventh trumpet is directed to the entire world—dragon, beast, and false prophet.

When the first trumpet sounded, symbolic hail, fire, and blood were cast upon the <u>earth</u>. The Goths under Alaric 395 AD descended on the apostate church. We must remember that at this stage of things, the church—state relationships made with Constantine were developing and would mature in the full apostasy in the year 538 AD See Uriah Smith *Prophecies of Daniel & the Revelation* pp. 476–478. When God's judgments fall on an apostate church, the nation that supports that church receives the brunt of His judgments. The trees and grass of the <u>third part</u>—papal dominated Western Europe were burnt up.

When the second trumpet of war sounded a symbolic mountain burning with fire fell into the <u>sea</u>. This represented the attacks by the Vandals under Genseric which came from the sea. The <u>third part</u> of the sea became blood probably representing the naval battles being fought. The <u>third part</u> of the ships were destroyed indicating naval encounters.

The third trumpet sounded and a great star symbolically fell from heaven. It fell upon the <u>third part</u> of the <u>rivers and upon the fountains of waters</u>. This prophecy was fulfilled in the furious attacks of Alaric and his Huns. Their attacks involved the Alps where the springs of waters originated. (See pp. 483–485 of *The Prophecies of Daniel and The Revelation).*

When the fourth trumpet sounded, the third part of the sun moon and stars were smitten. The last of the pagan Roman government was on its way out. Odoacer of the Heruli "…commanded that the office of Roman Emperor of the West should be abolished." The authorities bowed in submission to him. (See *The Prophecies of Daniel and The Revelation* by Uriah Smith pp. 485–489).

There were three trumpets yet to sound. The angel flying in the midst of heaven loudly proclaimed the last three trumpets to be woes. The results of these would be more devastating than <u>the previous four</u>.

SECTION 8

REVELATION CHAPTER 9

Chapter 9 of Revelation is a continuation of the prophesies of the trumpets.

When the fifth angel sounded, John saw a star fall from heaven unto the earth. To that star was given the key to the bottomless pit. "He" opened the bottomless pit and smoke came out of the pit to darken the sun. The star that fell was Chosroes of Persia. His fall opened the way for hoards of Saracens to descend on papal-dominated Rome. Mohomedanism darkened the sun of a false Christianity. The hoards of Saracens are described as "locust." Nahum 3:15 says, "…make thyself many as the locusts." Nahum 3:17 says, "Thy crowned are as the locust, and thy captains as the great grasshoppers…"—numerous!

They were commanded not to hurt the grass of the earth nor any green thing, nor the trees. They were to hurt only those men which have not the seal of God in their foreheads. Even though the "third part" is not specifically mentioned in this seal, it is evident that the target of this trumpet is still the papal system. They were to torment men for five months. This time period of five months (30x5 = 150 days or years) began on July 27, 1299. (See Uriah Smith's *The Prophecies of Daniel and The Revelation* pp. 504–505). Detailed interpretation of the individual verses of this chapter may be found in Uriah Smith's book *Prophecies of Daniel and The Revelation* pp. 493–505.

When the sixth trumpet sounded, a voice was heard "…saying to the sixth angel which had the trumpet, loose the four angels which are bound in the great river Euphrates. These Sultanies composing the Ottoman Empire (the Turks) were to continue for an hour, a day, a month and a year. Using the day-year principle, the Ottoman Empire was predicted to last for 391 years and 15 days. They were to slay the "third part" of men. John was given the number of the horse men—some two hundred thousand thousand.

From the heads of the horses issued fire, smoke and brimstone. This prophecy indicates the first use of firearms in battle. The "third part" of men were killed by the fire, smoke, and the brimstone.

Details of the verses of the sixth trumpet may be explored by reading *The Prophecies of Daniel and The Revelation* by Uriah Smith pp. 306–317.

The last two verses of Rev. 9 reads, "and the rest of the men which were not killed by these plagues yet <u>repented</u> not of the works of their hands, that they should not worship devils and idols of gold, and silver, and brass, and stone and of wood: which neither can see, nor hear, nor walk: neither <u>repented</u> they of their murders nor of their sorceries, nor of their fornication, nor of their thefts."

We see here God targeting an apostate church, a church, state union with His judgments, and yet they would not repent.

Using the day-year principle, Josiah Litch calculated the hour, day, month and a year prophecy and predicted that the Ottoman Empire, Turkey, would come to its end in August of 1840. A few days before August 11, 1840—the end of the 391 years 15 days—Josiah Litch predicted on the basis of the prophecy that the Turkish Empire would come to its end on specifically August 11, 1840. On that very day Turkey surrendered its power to the four great Christian powers of the West.

The demise of the Ottoman Empire (Turkey) occurred at precisely the time to fulfill the prophecy of the king of the North coming to his end and none shall help him. His former allies were the very ones to whom he was forced to submit thus ending the

Ottoman Empire. (See *Daniel's Difficulties Resolved* section 8 on Dan. 11).

Nothing is said of the apostate church under the fifth and sixth seals. However, a greater apostasy is predicted to take place during these times. This is detailed in the second and third repeats of the Revelation sequences. The deviation from truth is so wide off the mark, it is referred to as "abominations of the earth."

The rampaging of the Ottoman empire, God's judgment on the apostasy ended on August 11, 1840. We are, however still living in the time of the sixth trumpet. Abominations such as we have never seen before are creeping into the church.

Homosexual conduct is condoned by leaders of the false Christian churches. Sexual perverts are elected as ministers of the Gospel. Doctrines of devils are taught in the churches of the land.

The remaining time of the sixth trumpet will yet see the full force of God's judgments on the harlot system known as Babylon. (See section 17—Rev. chapter 18).

SECTION 9

REVELATION CHAPTER 10

Chapter 10 of Revelation contains events occurring during the time of the sixth trumpet and the sixth seal. John sees a mighty angel from heaven clothed with a cloud; a rainbow was on his head, and his face were as the sun; his feet as pillars of fire. His right foot was set upon the sea; His left foot was set on the earth. He had in his hand a little book opened. The words of the book of Daniel were shut up, and the book sealed even to the time of the end, Dan. 12:4. It would not be understood until the time of the end. In symbolic representation, the book of Daniel, held in the hand of the angel is now represented as open or understood.

The angel lifted his hand to heaven and swore by the creator of all things that there would be "...time no longer." All prophecies relating to time had now come to an end. The longest time prophecy which ended in 1844 AD was approaching after which there would be "time no longer." Rev. 10:7 says, "But in the days of the voice of the seventh angel <u>when</u> he shall <u>begin</u> to sound, the mystery of God should be finished..." the sounding of the seventh trumpet does not occur until Rev. 11:15. When the seventh angel begins to sound in Rev. 11:15 the mystery of God would be finished. Paul speaks of "...the mystery of the Gospel" in Eph. 6:19. John says that mystery (the Gospel) would be finished or probation is closed, when the seventh trumpet sounds.

A voice then spoke to John telling him to take the little book which was open in the hand of the angel and eat it up. It would be sweet in his mouth as honey, but it would make his belly bitter.

John did as he was told. He ate the little book. It was sweet in his mouth as honey but as soon as he had eaten it, it was bitter in his belly.

This illustration has its parallel in Eze. 3:1–4 "Moreover he said unto me, son of man, eat that thou findest; eat this roll and go speak unto the house of Israel. So I opened my mouth and he caused me to eat that roll. And he said unto me, son of man, cause thy belly to eat, and fill thy bowels with this roll that I give thee. Then did I eat it; and it was in my mouth as honey for sweetness. And he said unto me, son of man, go get thee unto the house of Israel, and speak with my words unto them."

When John the revelator ate the roll its sweetness illustrated the experience of those who expected Jesus to return in Oct 22, 1844—the end of the 2300 day prophecy. Misinterpreting the prophecy caused bitter disappointment when Jesus did not appear. The bitterness in John's belly illustrated the experience the church would undergo when their expectations were not realized.

God foresaw their dilemma, and placed it in prophetic record as an encouragement to His disappointed people even though they did not recognize it at the time.

The angel's words to John (to the disappointed believers) is, your work is not yet done, "…thou must prophesy again before many peoples, and nations and tongues, and kings." Rev. 10:11.

SECTION 10

REVELATION CHAPTER 11

Rev. 11 continues to give information on events that will occur during the sixth seal and the sixth trumpet. Rev. 11:1, 2 belongs to the end of chapter 10. Here the angel gives John a "...reed like unto a rod," and asks John to arise and measure the temple (sanctuary) of God, the altar and the worshipers. This is symbolic language, and does not refer to actual measurements. The angel is correcting the error that led to the great disappointment. He is saying rise and <u>consider</u> the temple (the heavenly sanctuary). They were considering the earth as the sanctuary to be cleansed (Dan. 8:14), hence the mistake in interpretation of the prophecy.

The angel goes on to say, "But the court which is without the temple leave out, and measure it not, for it is given unto the Gentiles." Heb. 13:12 says, "wherefore Jesus also, that He might sanctify the people with His own blood, suffered without the gate"—in the earth.

The angel is saying the earth is the court which is without the temple" leave out, and measure it not (do not consider it). It is in the hands of the Gentiles. Thus the correction is made by the angel.

The latter part of verse 2 starts a new train of thought. It takes us back to the 1260 years of papal persecution. The <u>holy city</u> mentioned in this verse refers to God's people. "And the holy city shall they tread under foot forty and two months." (See section 5 on Daniel chapter 8 for various terms used in scripture to

75

represent God's people). The forty and two months are the same as the 1260 years of papal supremacy. The people of God (the holy city) will be trodden under foot (persecuted) for 1260 years.

During that same period of time God's two witnesses (the old and new testaments) will prophesy clothed in sackcloth. The Old and New Testaments (the Holy Scriptures) were forbidden by the Roman church to be read, and in many cases were destroyed.

How do we know that the two witnesses are the word of God? The witnesses in verse four are "…the two olive trees, and the two candlesticks standing before the God of the earth." We go back to Zech. 4. Zechariah sees a candlestick in verse two. In verse three, he sees two olive trees one on each side of the candlestick. Zechariah asked the angel what that represented. (Zech 4:6) "Then he answered and spake unto me saying, this is the word of the Lord unto Zerubbabel, saying not by might, nor by power but by my spirit saith the Lord of host."

Rev. 11:4, "These are the two olive trees and the two candlesticks standing before the God of the earth." Thy word is a lamp unto my feet and a light (candlestick) unto my path. (Ps. 119:105).

Zechariah again asks the angel about the olive trees and the candlesticks. (Zech. 4:11–14). Verse 14 reads, "Then said he to me, these are the two anointed ones (the old and new testaments, (the New Testament mentioned here prophetically) that stand by the Lord of the whole earth."

Rev. 11:5 says, "And if any man will hurt them, (the word of God) fire proceeded out of their mouth, and devoured their enemies…" This is a reference to the word of God through Elijah to king Ahaziah, where the king sent to inquire of Baalzebub, the god of Ekron. Two captains and their fifties were consumed by fire at the word of Elijah. (See 2 Kings 1:9–12). Rev. 11:6 states that they (the word of God) "…have power to shut heaven that it rain not in the days of their prophecy." The word of God through Elijah, told wicked Ahab, that there would be neither dew nor rain until he said so. (See 1 Kings 17:1) The word of God also had

"...power over water to turn them to blood, and to smite the earth with all plagues, as often as they will." The reference is to the plagues that God's word brought upon Egypt against a stubborn Pharoah. (See Exodus 7–12).

Rev. 11:3 says that the two witnesses would prophesy 1260 years (a day for a year) clothed in sackcloth. Rev. 11:7 says, "and when they shall have finished their testimony (in sackcloth—the end of the 1260 years), the beast that ascended out of the bottomless pit shall make war against them, and shall overcome them and kill them." The prophecy brings us to the end of the 1260 years when Napoleon of France took the Pope prisoner; France became atheistic for at least 3½ years. The word of God was destroyed in public burnings.

Their dead bodies would lie in the street of the great city which spiritually is called Sodom (France gave license to all sorts of sexual spiritual improprieties) and Egypt, a society who openly defied God. (Rev. 11:8).

The prophecy states that the witnesses would be dead for three and a half days. A day for a year would be three and a half years. France openly embraced Atheism for exactly a period of three and a half years. The deadly results of legislating Atheism was seen in the chaos of the French Revolution. Three and a half years later, religion was reinstated and the Bible again given the respect it deserved.

Thereafter the British and foreign Bible society was formed, thus making Bibles available to the common people at large. Later the American Bible society was formed contributing to making the word of God the best selling book in the world today. Rev. 11:11, 12 illustrates the exalted position the word of God was predicted to achieve in our world today.

Rev. 11:13 speaks of a great earthquake and the tenth part of the city fell. France was one of the 10 divisions of the old Roman Empire. This verse probably refers to the terrible devastation resulting from the French Revolution.

The prophecy then skips to the sounding of the seventh trumpet. When this trumpet sounds "...the mystery of God should be finished..." (Rev. 10:7) and the kingdoms of this world would "...become the kingdoms of our Lord and of his Christ..." (Rev. 11:15).

It should be pointed out that between Rev. 11:13 and Rev. 11:14, a greater apostasy is yet to be developed. This apostasy is detailed in the second and third sequences of Revelation's prophecies.

When the seventh angel sounds, probation is closed. Verse 18 lists events to occur in chronological order.

1. The nations were angry—(the great time of trouble such as never was since there was a nation)

2. Thy wrath is come—(The seven last plagues. For in them is filled up the wrath of God)

3. And the time of the dead, that they should be judged—(the millennial judgment of the wicked)

4. Reward to God's servants the prophets and to the saints—("...and my reward is with me to give every man according as his works shall be." Rev. 22:12)

5. Destroy them that destroy the earth—(final destruction of the wicked Rev. 20)

SECTION 11

REVELATION CHAPTER 12

Rev. 12 begins the second repeat of the Revelation series. This chapter parallels Rev. 2 and 3—the seven churches. The thrust of the chapter is the identification and history of God's true church. Chapter 13 which follows, is a picture of the apostate Christian church. The pure woman of chapter 12 is in stark contrast to the harlot woman of Rev. 17.

In Rev. 12:1 the true church (Jer. 6:2) is clothed with the sun—the sun of Christ's righteousness (Mal 4:2). The moon is under her feet—the old dispensation which derived its illumination from the Christian era, was now in the past—under her feet. The crown of twelve stars represents the twelve apostles chosen to inaugurate the Christian dispensation.

She is pictured in verse two as being pregnant and about to deliver. Some have erroneously interpreted this woman to be Mary the mother of Jesus. This is a gross error when we consider that the woman fled into the wilderness where she is fed for 1260 years. It is further stated that the woman was persecuted for the same period of time. Mary does not fit the demands of the prophecy.

In Rev. 12, John sees a great red dragon having seven heads and ten horns. Seven crowns are seen on the <u>seven heads</u>. There are three seven-head-ten-horned beasts mentioned in the book of Revelation. Rev. 12 is the first one. Rev. 13 is the second—the leopard-like beast. Rev. 17 is the third—a scarlet colored beast full of the names of blasphemy. These three beasts all represent

Rome in various stages of its existence. The location of the crowns is significant. We will show that the crowns on the heads of the great red dragon of Rev. 12 represents Rome while the Caesars were ruling—Empire Rome. We will show that the crowns on the ten horns of the leopard-like beast of Rev. 13 represent Rome during the division of the empire into its ten parts. In Rev. 17 there are no crowns on either the heads nor the horns. The harlot woman is controlling the beast—religio-political Rome during the dark ages. The harlot woman is in control of the beast.

The great red dragon of Rev. 12:3 is primarily Satan "...that old serpent called the devil..." verse 9. Secondarily it is pagan (Empire Rome), and lastly Herod who sought the young child's life. Matt. 2:16. "...the dragon stood before the woman which was ready to be delivered, for to devour her child as soon as it was born."

Rev. 12:5 states that the woman brought forth a man child (Jesus) who was to rule all nations with a rod of iron. See Rev. 19:15 where Jesus will rule the nations with a rod of iron.

Little else is said of the man child. "...Her child was caught up to God, and to His throne." The reason for this is that the chapter is not on the work and ministry of Jesus, but on the identification and history of the woman—the true church of God.

The woman then flees to the wilderness where God prepared a place for her. She was fed and cared for a period of 1260 days or years.

The subject changes in verse 7. "...There was war in heaven: Michael (Christ) and His angels fought against the dragon (Satan) and the dragon fought and his angels."

In verse 8, Satan and his angels did not prevail. "Neither was their place found any more in heaven." In Job chapters 1 and 2, the sons of God came "...to present themselves before the Lord, and Satan came also among them." Apparently Satan was not debarred from presenting himself before the Lord, until Rev. 12:8 where after the crucifixion of the Son of God there was war in heaven "...Satan prevailed not." They were cast out and "...neither was their place found any more in heaven." They were permanently expelled from the presence of God. Verse 9 bears this out. The casting out is not the original casting out, simply because verse 9 states that Satan "...deceiveth the whole world; he was cast out into the earth, and his angels were cast out with him." Satan was jealous of Christ because he was left out of the counsels of God concerning the creation of this world. Apparently at the first expulsion from heaven this world and humankind in it was not yet created. Verse 10 lends support to this concept. "And I heard a loud voice saying in heaven, now (because of the casting out) is come salvation, and strength, and the kingdom of our God, and the power of His Christ; for (or because) the accuser of our brethren is cast down, which accused them before our God day and night." How could Satan be charged with being the accuser of our brethren at the first casting out if the controversy concerned the creation of this world which was apparently yet in the future?

Rev. 12:12 calls the heavens to rejoice apparently because Satan is no longer permitted contact with them. In contrast, "woe to the inhabitants of the earth and of the sea! For the devil is come down unto you (cast out and confined to this earth) having great wrath, because he knoweth that he hath but a short time."

Rev. 12:13 lends support to the war in heaven and the casting out of Satan being after his malignant crucifixion of the Son of God. It reads, "and when the dragon saw that he was cast unto the earth, he persecuted the woman which brought forth the man child." The persecution began "...when the dragon saw that he was cast unto the earth..." and the specific time of persecution is mentioned in the following verse 14, as a time, times, and half a time. This is clearly the 1260 years of papal supremacy and persecution of God's people mentioned twice in Daniel and five times in the book of Revelation. (References are Dan. 7:25, Dan. 12:7; Rev. 11:2; Rev. 11:3; Rev. 12:6; Rev. 12:14; Rev. 13:5).

81

Rev. 12:15 states that the serpent, the devil, cast out of this mouth water as a flood after the woman attempting to destroy her. If water represents peoples. multitudes, nations and tongues, certainly numerous people were used by the false Christian church during the dark ages in an attempt to rid the world of the pure woman—the true church of God.

But God intervened in verse 16. "And the <u>earth</u> helped the woman, and the <u>earth</u> opened her mouth, and swallowed up the flood (of persecution) which the dragon cast out of his mouth." This is an allusion to the rise of the beast which came up out of the <u>earth</u> (Rev. 13:11). The United States, the beast which came up out of the earth, became the haven for Christians, as this country recognized the rights of all peoples to live as their consciences dictated in matters of religion.

Verse 17 pictures the pure woman at the end of time. The dragon (or Satan) was wroth (angry) with the woman (the true church) "…and went to make war with the remnant (the last part) of her seed…" And the characteristics of that "remnant" are given. They keep the commandments of God—all ten! James 2:10 says, "for whosoever shall keep the whole law, and yet offend in one point, <u>he is guilty of all</u>." How many offend in the one point of the seventh-day Sabbath? The challenge comes from the Catholic church asking Protestants who profess the Bible as their source of doctrine, to show that Sunday keeping is a biblically valid doctrine. The evidence is not there.

The second characteristic of God's pure church is that they would "…have the testimony of Jesus Christ." Rev. 19:10 says, "…for the testimony of Jesus is the spirit of prophecy." The prophetic gift would be found in God's pure church.

To identify the pure woman of Rev. 12 we must look for the church which supports the keeping of all of God's Ten Commandments which includes the seventh-day Sabbath, and which has had the prophetic gift playing an important role in the establishment and functions of the organization.

There is one and only one church that meets both of these identification marks, and that is the Seventh-day Adventist Church. The church was called into existence by visions given over a period of more than seventy years. In the church's vaults are fabulous records of scenes past, present and future. The church has been given instruction as to political and religious developments to occur just prior to the end of all things. One statement that should concern our national leaders is given. When this nation shall enact laws enforcing the observance of Sunday, the first day of the week, a day for which there is no Biblical authority, God will consider the nation to be in national apostasy, <u>and national apostasy will be followed by national ruin</u>. Our legislators are not acquainted with these messages. They are not aware of the solemn and heavy responsibilities that rest upon their legislative decisions. May God help them!

SECTION 12

REVELATION CHAPTER 13

Rev. 13 is a somewhat parallel chapter to the seals. It is the second repeat of the apostasy that developed from a falling away from the principles of the true church.

In this chapter John stood on the sands of the sea and saw a beast rise up out of the sea. Rev. 17:15 states "…the waters which thou sawest where the whore sitteth, are peoples, and multitudes, and nations, and tongues."

This particular power arose from existing nations and is in contrast to another beast seen coming up out of the earth, Rev. 13:11. This latter beast develops from an area devoid of large masses of peoples, nations and tongues. This beast of Rev. 13:1–10 has also seven heads and ten horns—it is Rome. The crowns are on the 10 horns. Crowns represent the ruling authority. They are now on the horns. This is Rome during its division into the 10 kingdoms. We need to keep in mind that God considers Rome to exist until Jesus comes and puts an end to it. Dan. 7:11 speaking of the fourth beast with the little horn (Rome) says, "…I beheld even till the beast was slain and his body destroyed, and given to the burning flame." God will destroy Rome in the fires of perdition. The prophetic gift confirms that the papacy will continue till Jesus returns. In that way Rome is considered to continue till Jesus returns. Upon the heads of this beast was the name of blasphemy. What is blasphemy? (Mark 2:5–7) "When Jesus saw their faith, He said unto the sick of the palsy, son thy sins be forgiven thee, but there were certain of the scribes sitting there and reasoning in their hearts, why doth this man thus speak blasphemies? Who can forgive sins but God only?" These did not recognize that Jesus was indeed God in human flesh exercising His prerogative to forgive sins. Men forgiving sins raises questions as to the practice of the confessional in certain churches.

Another description of blasphemy is recorded in John 10:33, "The Jews answered Him saying, for a good work we stone thee not: but for blasphemy; and because that thou being a man, makest thyself God." Here again, Jesus' divinity was not recognized by the Jews. He was not blaspheming because He indeed was God in human flesh. This also raises serious questions as to the claims of the supreme leader of the Roman church. Blasphemy is described as a sinful mortal human being claiming characteristics that belong only to God.

The first beast of Rev. 13 had a body like unto a leopard. We recall the leopard beast of Dan. 1 which represented Greece. It had feet as the feet of a bear. This recalls the bear of Dan. 7 which represented Medo-Persia. It had the mouth of a lion. This recalls the lion of Dan. 7 representing Babylon. This is a composite beast, Rome, made up of the three preceding world empires. Dan. 7:11, 12 states that the fourth beast was destroyed and given to the burning flame. But as concerning the rest of the beasts, that is, Babylon, Medo-Persia and Greece, "...they had their dominion taken away, yet their lives were prolonged for a season and time." What the prophecy is saying is that when Babylon was conquered by Medo-Persia, the culture of Babylon was carried over into Medo-Persia for a time. When Medo-Persia fell to Greece, its culture was carried over into Greece for a season and a time. Similarly, when Greece fell to Rome, Grecian culture merged into the Roman Empire. The fourth beast, however, is considered to exist until Jesus puts an end to it in the fires of perdition. The dragon, or pagan Rome would give to this organization, its former power, his very seat of government (Rome) and great authority to rule, (Rev. 13:2). This verse parallels Dan. 11:31 where the "daily sacrifice" (the continuance of desolation)

Pagan Rome (see *Daniel's Difficulties Resolved*, chapter 8 on the "daily sacrifice") is taken away to make room for "…the abomination that maketh desolate," (papal Rome). Dan. 12:11 also affirms this transfer sequence. "And from the time that the "daily sacrifice" (pagan Rome) is taken away, and the "abomination that maketh desolate" (papal Rome) set up, there shall be a thousand two hundred and ninety days." Rev. 13:3 says that John saw one of his heads, as it were wounded to death. The question may be raised, which head? The reader is referred to comments on Rev. 17 where after the angel defines who the seven heads are, introduces an eighth head which was similar to the previous seven heads—pagan as the prior seven heads were. This eighth head will be shown to be the papacy. It is to this head that Berthier inflicted the deadly wound. The papal head was taken captive in 1798 where he died a prisoner in the custody of the French.

But the prophecy goes on to say, that the apparently deadly wound would be healed. Gradually after 1798 AD, there has been a resurgence of papal prominence. In 1929 AD Benito Mussolini restored to the papacy the real estate known as the Vatican. The deadly wound was healed. Thereafter "… all the world wondered after the beast." This suggests an unholy admiration of this power. The numerous travels of its present head and the adulation of millions around the world fulfills this prophecy to the letter.

Again, the blasphemous utterances of this beast power are brought to view in verse 5. He would continue dominance in religious and political things for forty-two months. Forty-two times thirty (the Jewish month) is the 1260 days (years). This is the time period allotted by prophecy to the papal system, a time beginning in 538 AD at the fall of the last Arian power the Ostragoths, and ending in 1798 when the pope was captured by Berthier and brought to France where he died a prisoner of that country.

Rev. 13:6 says that this power will blaspheme God by blaspheming His name. (See Uriah Smith's comments on

Revelation chapter 13). In assuming the title of Vicar of Christ, (see The Convert's Catechism of Catholic Doctrine pp. 28–30.) the pope is usurping the role of the only representative of Jesus on earth, which is the Holy Spirit. He is taking the place of God (the Holy Spirit) which, as a sinful created human being, he commits the sin of blasphemy as defined in the Word of God. He will also blaspheme God's tabernacle. At Christ's death on the cross, the veil of the temple was rent in two from the top to the bottom indicating that the Old Testament ritual of animal sacrifices which pointed to Jesus death on the cross, had now come to an end. However, the Roman Catholic system has introduced a new human priesthood shifting man's attention from Christ our Great High Priest in the heavenly sanctuary to gorgeous and extravagant cathedrals with immoral pastors leading the flock.

This power was predicted to "… make war with the saints, and to overcome them." The Roman Church knowingly or not has fulfilled the prophecy to the letter. Millions of God's faithful saints who chose not to follow the apostate Roman church were labeled "heretics," tortured and deprived of life by every inhumane method possible. It is difficult to understand why intelligent human being of this day and age would still be drawn to follow an organization of historically such a disreputable character!

And yet verse eight says, "…all that dwell upon the earth shall worship him, whose names are <u>not</u> written in the book of life of the Lamb slain from the foundations of the world."

Rev. 13:10 is an elaboration of verse 3. Verse 3 predicts that this beast would receive a deadly wound. Verse 10 says that "he that leadeth into captivity shall go into captivity; he that killeth with the sword will be killed with the sword."

In 1798 AD, as mentioned before, Bertheir took the pope prisoner where he died a captive of the French government. This seriously curtailed the power of the papacy to injure the church of God and the true followers of Jesus Christ.

Just about the time the first beast (the leopard-like beast) was taken captive, John saw another beast "...coming up out of the earth." The only country rising to political significance, at that time was the United States of America. The United States declared its independence from Britain in the year 1776. Just 22 years later, the Roman power received its "deadly wound"—1798. The United States did not develop from previously populated areas of nations. It came into being by people migrating to this sparsely populated land to develop it and to flee religious intolerance common in the old world. It certainly arose "from the earth"—not from "...peoples and multitudes, and nations, and tongues."

This latter beast had two horns like a lamb. If horns represents power, we may consider the power of this country and its greatness to have grown out of the separation of church and state, a distinct difference from old world countries which were ruled by church dominated governments. Church dominated countries invariably resort in one way or another to the persecution of dissenting citizens. Fear, lack of freedom, a sense of being a "second class" citizen, dampens, inventiveness, smothers free thinking, and stifles the rapid progress of a nation towards greatness.

This latter beast with the lamb-like horns (the United States) would eventually speak like a dragon. The term "dragon" is first used in Rev. 12:3. Verse 9 says,"...and the great dragon was cast out, that old serpent, called the devil and Satan..." In verse four, "...the dragon stood before the woman which was ready to be delivered, for to devour her child as soon as it was born." We will recall the story of Herod's attempt to destroy Jesus as recorded in Matt. 2. The dragon represents primarily Satan, secondarily pagan Rome, and thirdly Herod, the tool used in the attempt on the Christ child's life.

How will this country speak as a dragon? When this country shall repudiate the principles of its constitution as a Protestant and Republican form of government, and shall enact laws enforcing religious observances which have no sanctions in the Word of God, but whose origins date back to pagan customs of ancient Rome, and even further back to ancient Babylon, then will God consider this nation to be in national apostasy, and the warning from God is that national ruin will follow.

Rev. 13:12 shows a decided straying from the separation of church and state. "and he exerciseth all the power of the first beast before him"—the one described in Rev. 13:1–10.The first beast was a religio-political combination which forced worship on pain of death to dissenters.

The rest of verse 12 confirms this deviation from that which made this nation great. It reads, "…and causeth the earth and them that dwell therein to worship the first beast, whose deadly wound was healed." Here again we have a government-forced religion, which directs worship, not to God, but to the first beast whose deadly wound was healed. When this occurs, authentic information from God indicates that God's blessing on this nation will be withdrawn and national ruin will follow.

Rev. 13:13 is startling. "And he doeth great wonders…" Because of this nation's guarantee of freedom, scientific wonders have proliferated from sea to shining sea. One specific wonder mentions "…so that he maketh fire come down from heaven on the earth in the sight of men." Is this prophecy fulfilled in the Hiroshima and Nagasaki incident? After all, this is the only country to have dared to activate such a destructive instrument. The known worldwide consequences of atomic radiation may have been a deterrent on other nations using these weapons.

In verse 13, this country would be involved in "great wonders." In verse 14, it would be involved with "miracles." Are the "wonders" of verse 13, the same as the "miracles" of verse 14?

We may look at scientific wonders as outstanding achievements with a solid rational explanation for the accomplishments. Miracles on the other hand may be seen as accomplishments for which there is no scientific or rational explanation for the results.

This country will be, and is in the process of fulfilling this prophecy to the letter. The scientific accomplishments of this nation can hardly be disputed. The increasing involvements of this nation with the occult, not only with séances, Satanism and contacts with the "dead," but also with peripheral practices such as palm readings, horoscopes, astrology and the likes, are preparing this nation to accept deceptions as truth in the place of facts. Truly this county will deceive "…them that dwell on the earth by the means of those miracles which he had power to do in the sight of the beast." (Rev. 13:14).

Rev. 13:14 points also to this power, the lamb-like beast (the United States) saying to the people of the earth that "…they should make an image (a likeness) to the beast (the first beast of Rev. 13:1–10), which had the wound by a sword and did live." The wording of this latter passage is compatible with our form of government. A monarchy or a dictatorial government issues laws from the ruler or dictator. This second beast says to the people that "they should make an image to the beast…"—a Republican form of government. Government of the people by the people, for the people.

An image is a likeness of. This country of ours will be asking the people to make an image or a likeness of the first beast. The first beast (Rev. 13:1–10) was a religio-political combination—Roman Catholicism using the arm of the state to force compliance of its citizen's to the dogmas of the church many of which had no foundation in scriptural truth.

This is dire prophecy for this country which was the shining example to the world of what religious liberty could do for the social advantages of its citizenry. Furthermore, Rev. 13:15 says, "…he had power to give life unto the image of the beast." In other words, to activate the image of the former religio-political organization; that activation would be such that those who "… would not worship (not God but) the image of the beast…should be killed." Enforced worship on pain of death is a retrogression to the days of the Catholic inquisition, when horrible inhumanities were practiced on religious dissenters in the name of religion.

Then the prophecy comes to the famous verse dealing with the mark of the beast—the beast of Rev. 13:1–10. The beast of Rev. 13:1–10 is Rome; but it is Rome, not in its pagan (empire) from, but Rome during the division of the empire into its ten parts. The crowns (the ruling power) are on the ten horns of the leopard-like beast of Rev. 13. This is Rome during the division of the empire into its ten parts and specifically it speaks of Rome in its papal form.

Rev. 13:16 says that the second beast of Rev. 13 will cause all, "...both small and great, rich and poor, free and bond, to receive a mark in their right hand or in their foreheads."

What is this mark, and what is the purpose of the mark? First, the purpose of the mark is to boycott those who do not have the mark of the beast. Rev. 13:17 says, "...and that no man might buy or sell, save he that had the mark..." This country has practiced sanctions on uncooperative countries to a fine art. You may neither buy nor sell to them unless they comply with our regulations. It is predicted that this type of boycott, internal sanctions on its citizens, will be practiced on those who would not accept the mark of the beast; those who will not accept the name of the beast (those who refuse membership in the ranks of this religio-political organization), or those who refuse to recognize the number of the name, or title of the beast.

Rev. 13:17 reads, "and that no man night buy or sell, save he that had the mark, or the name of the beast, or the number of his name."

Now, what is the mark of the beast of Rev. 13:1–10? The beast of Rev. 13:1–10 is a religious organization. Rev. 13:4 says, "...and they <u>worshipped</u> the beast, saying who is like unto the beast?" Verse 8 says, "and all that dwell upon the earth shall <u>worship</u> him, whose names are not written in the book of life of the lamb slain from the foundation of the world." This is a religious organization—one calling on people to <u>worship</u>.

We call attention to this nation' calling people to the recognition and worship, not of God, but the organization represented by the beast of Rev. 13:1–10. What is the mark of this organization? The mark of "authority" of this organization, the Roman Catholic church, is the change of God's seventh day Sabbath to Sunday, the first day of the week.

No scriptural passage has given this church license to change God's Sabbath, the seventh day of the week to Sunday the first day of the week.

Uriah Smith quotes from "The Catholic Christian Instructed:"

Question:"Have you any other way of proving that the church has power to institute festivals of precepts?"

Answer:"Had she not such power, she could not have done that in which all modern religionist agree with her—she could not have substituted the observance of Sunday, the first day of the week, for the observance of Saturday, the seventh day, a change for which there is no scriptural authority."

In Dan. 7:25 this same church is predicted to <u>think</u> to change times and laws—"of the most high" is implied by the preceding parts of the verse.

So this church has itself claimed that the altering of God's law is its mark of ecclesiastic authority—Saturday to Sunday.

The seal of God (see chapter seven, section 6 of this book) is the seventh day Sabbath. The seal is symbolically placed in the foreheads of those who willingly accept and observe God's seventh day Sabbath. In contrast, the mark of the beast is placed in the foreheads (the thinking deciding portion of the brain) of those who follow and accept the spurious Sabbath of papal origin. We will notice that in Rev. 13:16 the mark is placed either in the right hand or the foreheads of those who do follow the beast. When religious laws are enforced, and particularly laws enforcing Sunday observance, many secularist will comply, refraining from work on Sunday in compliance with the law, even though they may not conscientiously be in agreement with it. They receive the mark symbolically in the right hand. The seal of God (the seventh day Sabbath) is placed in the forehead alone. It is a voluntary acceptance of God's seventh-day Sabbath, the memorial of His creation.

To reemphasize Rev. 13:17, there are three things, any one of which may exempt one from the prohibitions of buying or selling. These are:

1.Having the mark of the beast—a Sunday observer. When this nation enforces Sunday observance.

2.The name of the beast. A member of the Catholic faith.

3.The number of his name.

Numbers 1 and 2 have been mentioned above. What is number 3—the number of his name? First, what is the name of the beast? Rev. 13:18 says the number of the beast is the number of a man. Verse 17 says the number is found in his name. What is his name? We must assume that this is not a single human being since the power referred to has a history of existence over the centuries. It must be therefore the name or title assumed by the successive leaders of this organization. The title assumed by the popes of this organization is "Vicar of Christ." (See the Convert's Catechism Doctrine pp. 28, 30). In the Latin, Vicar of Christ is "Vicarius Filii Dei."

In number three, above, you may escape sanctions if you have the number of his name. You may escape sanctions, if you acknowledge the number of the beast, which is the number of a man, the number being found in his name. By acknowledging the number of his name, you acknowledge that he is the Vicar or representative of Christ. The only scriptural representative of Christ is the Holy Ghost sent by Jesus from above. Blasphemy is usurping the role of God the Holy Spirit.

The number found in his name, or title, is given in Rev. 13:18 as "six hundred three score and six or 666. It should be pointed out that 666 is not the mark of the beast as is so often erroneously suggested. Six hundred and sixty six is the number in the name or title of the man who represents the beast of Rev. 13:1–10, whereas the mark of the beast is the enforcement of Sunday observance which Roman Catholicism claims as the mark of her authority.

Let us look at the claimed title of the head of the Roman church, "Vicar of Christ." In the Latin it is "Vicarius Filli Dei." Rev. 13:18 "Here is wisdom. Let him that hath understanding count the number of the beast (the organization which the beast represents) for it is the number of a man; and his number is six hundred three score and six.

$$
\begin{array}{rl}
V = & 5 \\
I = & 1 \\
C = & 100 \\
A = & \\
R = & \\
I = & 1 \\
U = & 5 \\
S = & \\
F = & \\
I = & 1 \\
L = & 50 \\
I = & 1 \\
I = & 1 \\
D = & 500 \\
E = & \\
I = & 1 \\
\hline
& 666
\end{array}
$$

We hear negative minds showing that this name or that name also adds up to 666. What should be clearly evident is that these alternate name suggestions do not fit the other details of the prophecy. The papal system fits every detail of the prophetic description. We hear argument as to whether the title Vicarius Filli Dei was really on the pope's triple crown or tiara. Arguments such as these miss the point. The head of that organization claims the title of Vicar of Christ, and that is sufficient evidence to show that the prophecy is correctly interpreted.

Going back to Rev. 13:12 we find the lamb-like beast "...causeth the earth and them which dwell therein to worship the first beast, whose deadly wound was headed." The statement seems mild at first reading but there is a sense of coercion, or force in the statement. "...Causeth them which dwell...to worship..." This is forced religion as the world experienced during the dark ages. Verse 15 confirms this in the chilling language of "...and cause that as many as would not worship the image of the beast should be killed."

To worship the beast is one way of receiving the mark (Sunday observance when enforced) which would exempt you from the ban on buying and selling.

It should be emphasized that no one receives the mark of the beast today. This occurs only when this country by the direction of its national legislative bodies forces the observance of Sunday the false Sabbath for which there is no scriptural evidence. Then will God consider this county to be in national apostasy and prophecy of a most reliable sort, says, "national ruin will follow."

It should be pointed out here that there are two massive forces that are shaping up for an earth shaking confrontation. The first is already mentioned above. This country will lead the world to worship the first beast and its image.

The second massive force confronts the first in Rev. 14:9, 10. It reads, "And the third angel followed them, saying with a loud voice, (this is an announcement from God). If any man worship the beast (Roman Catholicism) and his image, (the church-state combination that this nation will develop) and receive his mark in his forehead, or in his hand, the same shall drink of the wine of the wrath of God, (Rev. 15:1 "…the seven last plagues; for in them is filled up the wrath of God") which is poured out without mixture (no mercy) into the cup of His indignation; and he shall be tormented with fire and brimstone in the presence of the holy angels, and in the presence of the Lamb." Who wins this confrontation? There is no guessing as to the outcome.

SECTION 13

REVELATION CHAPTER 14

This chapter is inserted between chapter 13 (the apostasy) and God's judgments on the apostasy because of the dire warning of the third angel's message. In Rev. 13:12 this country will cause "…the earth and them that dwell therein to worship (not God but) the first beast, whose deadly wound was healed." Furthermore in Rev. 13:15, he will "…cause that as many as would not worship the image of the beast (the church-state combination prophesied to be formed in this country) should be killed.

The worship contrast comes a little later. John first sees in vision the 144,000 standing on Mount Zion. They sing a new song before the throne of God—a song of their experience. None can sing that song but the 144,000. In heaven even the lyrics of the song must reflect the truth of a person's experience.

John says, he saw another angel (a messenger) symbolically fly in the midst of heaven. He had the everlasting gospel to preach to all that dwell on the earth. Every nation, kindred, tongue and people. This is a symbolic representation of the very last warning preached to a dying world.

The message is in stark contrast to the call of the two-horned beast to worship either the beast whose deadly wound was healed (Rev. 13:12) or the image of the beast (Rev. 13:15). The first angel's message is a call to love and glorify God because we are now living in the time of the great judgment hour of God, and we are therefore called to worship—not the beast nor his image—but the God who created "…the heaven and the earth, and the sea and the fountains of waters." The latter part of this quote is a take off on the Sabbath commandment and is a call to relinquish Sunday worship, a Roman Catholic tradition, for which there is no Biblical authorization, and worship God on His seventh day Sabbath. The Roman church (in the <u>Catholic Mirror</u> Sept 2, 1893, Sept 9,1893, Sep 16,1893, Sept 23,1893) has openly challenged the Protestant community who claim to follow the Bible and the Bible only, to prove from scripture their reason for Sunday observance. The Roman Catholic church states that the evidence is not there. They refuted all evidence used by Protestants to vindicate Sunday as a Christian day of worship. The Roman church frankly admits that Sunday observance is a matter of their own doing.

John then sees another angel (another messenger). His message introduces the term "Babylon" for the first time. The description of this term is not given until Rev. 17:5. However, who or whatever "Babylon" is the angel says, it is "fallen." This is not literal Babylon. Indeed literal Babylon was destroyed and has never been rebuilt. Why is Babylon fallen? The text says, "<u>Because</u> she made all nations drink of the wine of the wrath of her fornication." We will see in the comments on Rev. 17 that Babylon is represented as a harlot woman. A woman in symbolic scripture represents a church (see Jer 6:2). The pure woman of Rev. 12 is God's true Christian church. In contrast, the harlot woman of Rev. 17 is the apostate Christian church. She gave birth to harlot daughter churches—the numerous protestant churches all claiming to be teaching correct doctrine but still clinging to remnants of Catholicism—including Sunday observance. "Babylon" then in Rev. 17:5 is the mother church <u>and</u> her harlot daughter churches.

The prophecy says, she is fallen <u>because</u> she made all nations drink (or become spiritually drunk) of the wine (the false doctrine) of her fornication. Her husband is supposed to be Christ. She has left her husband, Christ, and has made the world drunk with her false doctrines.

It should be pointed out here that there are four names that you will see in the book of Rev. that all mean the same thing. These are:

1.The beast and the image of the beast in Rev. 13

2.The beast and the false prophet introduced in Rev. 16

3.Babylon Rev. 17:5

4.Harlot mother church and harlot daughters. Rev. 17:5

Both 3 and 4 are introduced in Rev. 17. They all refer to Roman Catholicism and apostate Protestantism.

The foregoing terms all point to an apostate Christianity consisting of the Roman church and a wide array of Protestant churches all claiming to be teachers of God's word but who have strayed from its divine precepts. The word "Babylon" comes from "Babel" where there was confusion of languages and is a fit representation of the confusion of doctrines seen in the "Christian" churches of the day.

Then the dire warning of the third angel. This country, the lamb-like beast of Rev. 13:11–18 calls on the world to worship the beast and the image of the beast. Rev. 14:9–12 warns "If any man worships the beast and his image, and receives his mark in his forehead or in his hand, the same shall drink of the wine of the wrath of God, (The wine of the wrath of God is the plagues of Rev. 16. (See also Rev. 15:1) "…seven angels having the seven last plagues; for in them is filled up the wrath of God), which is poured out without mixture (not mixed with mercy) into the cup of his indignation; and he shall be tormented with fire and brimstone in the presence of the holy angels, and in the presence of the Lamb."

Rev. 14:11, "And the smoke of their torment ascendeth up forever and ever." The smoke of earth's final conflagration will dissipate into outer space for ever and ever. "…and they have no rest day nor night, who worship the beast and his image, and whosoever receiveth the mark of his name." The explanation of this verse will be dealt with in the discussion of the final eradication of sin in the fires kindled for sinners in the last days recorded in Rev. 19 and 20.

Suffice it to say, at this time that this text is not to be interpreted as an eternal burning hell fire in which people suffer eternally. Eze. 28:18 says, that God will "...bring forth a fire from the midst of thee (Satan). It shall devour thee and I will bring thee to ashes upon the earth in the sight of all them that behold thee..." Again in Mal. 4:3 the prophet says, "And ye shall tread down the wicked; for they shall be ashes under the soles of your feet..." It is reasonable that if Satan is brought to ashes, so will his followers be brought to ashes also.

Rev. 14:12 gives the characteristics of God's saints "...they...keep the commandments of God (including the seventh day Sabbath) and the faith of Jesus."

John's attention is then turned to a symbolic representation of the second coming of Jesus. He sees one like the Son of Man sitting on a cloud, having a golden crown on His head and a sharp sickle in His hand. He is told by another angel to "thrust in thy sickle, and reap for the time is come for thee to reap for the harvest of the earth is ripe" The Son of Man then thrust in His sickle "...and the earth was reaped."

Another angel was seen coming out of the temple, also with a sharp sickle. And still another angel came out which had power over fire. He cried to the prior angel with the sickle to thrust in his sickle to gather the clusters of the vine. A symbolic representation of the end of the wicked is represented in Rev. 14:20.

SECTION 14

REVELATION CHAPTER 15

John is given a vision of seven angels having the seven last plagues; these will be poured out before Jesus returns.

However, John is projected in vision into the future and is shown a sea of glass mingled with fire. He sees those who had gotten the victory over the beast, and his image, and over this mark. They were seen standing on the sea of glass. They had harps. They sang the song of Moses and of the Lamb. They glorified God for His marvelous works. His justice and truth is also mentioned.

John says, "…and after that I looked and behold the temple of the tabernacle of the testimony in heaven was opened." The "after that" in this verse does not mean that after he saw those who had gotten the victory over the beast, the image to the beast, and over the number of his name, the event he was about to mention took place. He sees the seven angels coming out of the temple with the seven last plagues. Obviously the plagues take place before God's people are glorified and admitted to heaven. One of the four beast (living creatures) gave unto the seven angels, seven golden vials—full of the wrath of God. This short chapter gives some sanctuary images as a prelude to God's judgments on the apostasy. The apostasy which has and is developing in the Christian world during the sixth seal and the sixth trumpet is so deviant that God designated it as "abominations of the earth." It is not difficult to see the appropriateness of this description when we hear of homosexual marriages, homosexual "ministers," abortions, ministers who do not believe the sacred scriptures (communications with the "dead") and a host of teachings having no basis whatever in the Word of God.

SECTION 15

REVELATION CHAPTER 16

In this chapter John heard a great voice coming from the temple telling the seven angels to go their ways and pour out the vials of God's wrath upon the earth.

It is important for the reader to understand that the book of Revelation is a book about Christianity. It is a book that contrasts, in a way, the true church (genuine Christianity), from the false church(es) (false Christianity). It depicts God's judgments upon a church claiming to represent Him, but totally distorting truth from its position of reality. When we grasp this concept clearly in mind, Revelation takes on a clarity not seen when a lot of convoluted spiritualizing is woven around the prophetic texts.

Rev. 16 is a chapter on God's judgments on Babylon the false Christian system mentioned in Rev. 17. This may seem a deviation from the concept held by many that the plagues are poured out on all the wicked of the word. Let us examine the evidence. Ellen White made the statement that the plagues are not universal. Let us keep in mind the four terms used in Revelation that mean the same thing.

1. The beast and the image of the beast in Rev. 13

2. The beast and the false prophet introduced in Rev. 16

3. Babylon

4. Harlot mother church and harlot daughters.

These all refer to Catholicism and apostate Protestantism.

Now let us look at the plague chapter of Rev. 16. The first angel pours his vial upon the earth. A noisome and grievous sore develops upon <u>the men which had the mark of the beast and upon those who worshipped his image.</u>

The men who had the mark of the beast and those who worshipped his image, are men of spiritual Babylon.

The second angel poured his vial upon the sea and it became <u>as</u> the blood of a dead man. All living creatures died in the sea. This bloody plague does not end here but is extended into plague three. The third angel poured his vial upon the rivers and fountains of waters, and they also became blood.

Then the reason for the bloody plagues is given. Verses 5 & 6 say, "…thou art righteous, O Lord, which art, and wast, and shall be, because thou hast judged thus, for <u>they</u> have shed <u>the blood of saints and prophets</u>, and thou hast given them blood to drink; for they are worthy." Who are the "they" of verse 6? We turn to Rev. 18:24 and read "And in her, (Babylon) was found <u>the blood of prophets and of saints</u>, and of all that were slain upon the earth."

The first three plagues are thus seen to be directed to Babylon—the system of false Christianity.

The fourth angel poured his vial upon the sun; and power was given to the sun to scorch men with fire. This is the only plague in which Babylon is not in any way singled out. The effects of this plague will be universal. Speaking of the 144,000, Rev. 7:16 reads, "They shall hunger no more, neither thirst any more; neither shall the sun light on them, nor any heat." Apparently the 144,000 will suffer the inconvenience of the heat of the fourth plague, but God will preserve them through it.

The fifth angel poured out his vial on the <u>seat of the beast</u>, and his kingdom was full of darkness. Is this a literal darkness or is it only a symbolic spiritual darkness? The seat of the beast is Rome, the origin of Catholicism. Rome is already the seat and origin of spiritual darkness so what would be the intent of the prophecy to state what already is. We look at Ex. 10:22 where "… Moses stretched forth his hand toward heaven; and there was a thick darkness in all the land of Egypt three days." If God could cover Egypt with supernatural darkness, is His hand short today that He could not do likewise to Rome? If this were done, how significant an act of God would this be to point out the Mother church as the great problem of the Christian spiritual world!

"...The sixth angel poured out his vial upon the great river Euphrates; and the water thereof was dried up." Here the waters represent peoples, multitudes, nations and tongues which support the Babylon system. When the literal waters of the Euphrates were dried up by Cyrus, Babylon fell. The process by which literal Babylon fell, is used to illustrate the fall of spiritual Babylon. Deep into the plague chapter of Revelation when people realize that they are eternally lost, they will turn on their ministers, the false shepherds, and will slay them.

"The people see they have been deluded. They accuse one another of having led them to destruction; but all unite in heaping their bitterest condemnation upon the <u>ministers</u>. Unfaithful <u>pastors</u> have prophesied smooth things; they have led their hearers to make void the law of God and to persecute those who would keep it holy. We (the lay people) are lost!—they cry and you are the cause of our ruin; and they turn upon the false shepherds. The work of destruction begins among those who have professed to be the spiritual guardians of the people. The false watchmen are the first to fall!" (*Great Controversy* pp. 655, 656).

Destroy the hierarchy and what is left of the system? Nothing! Spiritual Babylon falls!

The sixth plague goes on to say, "...the water thereof was dried up, that the way of the kings of the East might be prepared." The drying up of the water prepares the way for that which follows.

What follows is circumstances which culminates in the Battle of Armageddon. It starts with the introduction of three unclean spirits, like frogs, coming out of the mouth of the dragon (false teachings from pagan/non-Christian religions of the world), and out of the mouth of the beast (of Rev. 13:1–10 false teachings from the mouth of Catholicism) and out of the mouth of the false prophet (false teachings from the mouth of apostate Protestantism). Rev. 16:14 says, "For they are the spirits of devils, working miracles which go forth unto the kings of the earth and of the whole world, (dragon, beast and false prophet) to gather them to the battle of that great day of God Almighty." Rev. 16:16 goes on to say, "And he gathered them together into a place called in the Hebrew tongue, Armageddon."

What confusion we see in writings on the subject of Armageddon! God has given us undisputed instruction as to what Armageddon is!

"The Battle of Armageddon is soon to be fought. He on whose vesture is written the name, King of Kings and Lord of Lords, leads forth the armies of heaven on white horses; clothed in fine linen, clean and white." (MS 172, 1899. SDA Bible Commentary, vol. 7 p 982)

Where is the above word picture taken from? It is to be found in Rev. 19:16. It takes only a kindergarten mentality to see that God's servant is saying that Rev. 19:11–21 is a detailed description of Armageddon and its eventual outcome. In fact Armageddon goes further than Rev. 19. It included all of chapter 20 also.

We will notice that the kings of the earth and of the whole world would be gathered to the battle of the great day of God Almighty which battle is called in the Hebrew tongue Armageddon. (Rev. 16:14–16). We put that together with Rev. 19:19 where "…the beast and the kings of the earth, and their armies gathered together to make war against Him that sat on the horse (Jesus) and against His army."

The final results of Armageddon are given in Rev. 19:20, 21.

Rev. 16:17 records the pouring out of the seventh vial. The vial is poured out into the air. A voice is heard saying, it is done. Verse 18 speaks of voices, and thunderings, and lightenings; and a great earthquake, so great an earthquake such as never was since men were upon the earth. This was followed with great hail every stone weighing about a talent. Rev. 16:19 reiterates the division of the world of the unsaved into three parts. The three parts are the same as Rev. 16:13—the dragon, beast and the false prophet.

SECTION 16

REVELATION CHAPTER 17

Rev. 17 represents the third repeat sequence of the book. The true church is omitted in this sequence even as Babylon is omitted in the last two repeats of the Daniel series.

Following Rev. 16, John is taken back in time by one of the angels which had the seven vials. He was called to see the judgment of "...the great whore that sitteth on many waters"—the false Christian church(es), that are supported by many peoples, multitudes, nations, and tongues.

The angel carried John away in the spirit into the wilderness. John saw a woman arrayed in purple and scarlet and decked with gold and precious stones, and pearls. She was sitting on a scarlet colored beast, full of the names of blasphemy. The beast had seven heads and ten horns. It is noteworthy that this beast does not have crowns on the heads or on the horns. This is Rome during the dark ages when the church controlled the state. This woman had in her hand a golden cup filled with abominations and filthiness of her fornications. This woman is in sharp contrast to the pure woman of Rev. 12.

On the woman's forehead was written Mystery, Babylon the Great, The Mother of Harlots and Abominations of the Earth. The mother church is Roman Catholicism which is pictured as giving birth to daughter churches, (Protestant churches) which were also harlot churches by their clinging to the errors propagated by the mother church.

Between the mother church and its harlot daughters we have such teachings as Sunday sacredness; the worship of Mary; the worship of saints; the teaching of the immortality of the soul; the teaching of an eternal burning hell fire; the secret rapture; unknown tongues; infant baptism; perverted methods of baptism; salvation by works; penance; purgatory; confession to priests instead of confession to God; and now we add additional abominations such as sanctioning of the gay and lesbian life styles, homosexual marriages, homosexual ministry; the condoning of the occult, such as communication with the "dead"; psychics of all sorts; astrology; and the list goes on.

The prophet goes on to say, in verse 6, "And I saw the woman drunk (stupefied) with the blood of the saints, and with the blood of the martyrs of Jesus." Anyone who knows anything about the Roman church knows that her history is written indelibly with the blood of God's saints. John marveled.

In Rev. 17:7 the angel said to John, why do you marvel? "I will tell thee the mystery of the woman, and of the beast that carrieth her, which hath the seven heads and ten horns."

In verse 8 the angel says, the beast that thou sawest "…was, and is not." We go to the end of the verse where the angel adds "…and yet is." The "…and yet is" should be understood whenever we run across the phrase "was, and is not." The beast that "was and is not" is pagan (empire) Rome which was in the past and no longer exists as such at the time the prophecy is refer-ring to. The "…and yet is" applies to Rome in its papal form. Pagan Rome was, and is not, yet it exists in papal Rome.

It shall ascend out of the bottomless pit, a term that usually applies to things having a Satanic origin. It will go into perdition. Rome will last till Jesus puts an end to it in the fires of perdition. Those whose names are not written in the book of life shall wonder. This ties in with the latter part of Rev. 13:3, "…and all the world wondered after the beast."

In verse 9 the angel says, "and here is the mind which hath wisdom. The seven heads are seven mountains, on which the woman sitteth." The next verse says in the King James version, "and there are seven kings."

Uriah Smith points out that in the ancient manuscripts the "there are seven kings" should be translated "...and are seven kings." The Modern Language Version translates this verse as "they also are seven kings." The Revised Standard Version translates this as, "...they are also seven kings."

Let us go back to the King James Version, "The seven heads are seven mountains, on which the woman sitteth, and are seven kings."

The angel goes on, "Five are fallen (or are in the past. When a king "stands up" he takes the kingdom to rule (see Dan. 11:2, 3 and Dan. 12:1). When he dies, he is fallen) and one is..." one is presently ruling. Remember in verse 7 the angel tells John, "... I will tell thee the mystery of the woman and of the beast that carrieth her..." When the angel says,"...and one is" it must refer to present tense in John's day. The "and one is," is the king ruling in John's day. That king was Emperor Domitian. Now how do we determine who the previous five kings are? If we use the principle of omitting the minor kings as in Dan. 2 and Dan. 11 (see *Daniel's Difficulties Resolved* on chapter 2 and 11) we arrive at five major kings before Emperor Domitian, These are Augustus Caesar, Tiberius Caesar, Claudius Caesar (these three are mentioned in Luke 2 and 3 and Acts 11 and 18), Nero, and Vespasian. (see the World Book Encyclopedia vol. 16 page 392)

Here we have the five fallen kings plus the "one is," Emperor Domitian, accounting for six major kings. The verse continues, "...and the other is not yet come." The seventh is still in the future to John's day. Who is the seventh head or king? If we look at the list of Roman Emperors following Domitian (see The World Book Encyclopedia vol16 page 392) we find 34 listed. Then in the year 283 AD the empire was divided into East and West with emperors of the East and West listed. How does one pick the seventh head from this sizable list of Emperors? The very last Emperor before the "decline and fall of Rome" was a man by the name of Constantine the Great. He had the second longest reign of any emperor (30 years). The only one with a longer reign was Augustus Caesar (41 years). Furthermore, Constantine was able to again reunite the Eastern and the Western divisions of the empire under his singular rule. It is not difficult to see Constantine the Great filling the role of the seventh head of the prophecy.

The prophecy concerning the seventh head (Rev. 17:10) goes on to say, "…and when he cometh, he must continue a short space." This is not to say, that the seventh head would continue a short space. He indeed reigned for 30 years. It means that the empire he ruled was on its way out.

Constantine the Great ruled from 307 to 337 AD The World Book Encyclopedia vol. 16 p 392 lists the "decline and fall of Rome" starting with the death of Constantine in the year 337 AD and the prophecy is fulfilled to the letter.

Rev. 17:11 says, "And the beast that was, and is not, (and "yet is" is to be understood) even he, (the papal head) is the eight, and is of the seven (he is pagan as the previous seven), and goeth into perdition." It is the papal part of Rome that will exist until Jesus destroys it in the fires of perdition. It is this head, the papal head which received the deadly wound.

Rev. 17:12 calls attention to the ten horns. The angel says, they "are ten kings which have received no kingdom as yet." As the angel spoke to John (AD 96), the division of the Roman Empire into its ten parts was yet in the future.

The text goes on to say, "…but receive power as kings one hour with the beast." Uriah Smith points out that the original meaning of "…one hour with the beast" is that they will rule simultaneously with each other—at the same time. This is in contrast to the heads which are successive—one following the other.

Rev. 17:13 continues. Speaking of the ten horns (the 10 divisions of the Roman Empire), they will have "…one mind, and shall give their power and strength unto the beast." They will support the beast (the church-state combination) which in the next verse (verse 14) will "...make war with the Lamb." They make war with the lamb by persecuting His people.

Rev. 17:16 reveals a change taking place in the attitude of the ten horns. They will eventually "...hate the whore, and shall make her desolate, and naked, and shall eat her flesh and burn her with fire." This prophecy fits the development of the Protestant Reformation which severely curtailed the work of the Roman Church.

Rev. 17:17 confirms this support-then-turn-against attitude of the ten horns. It says, "For God hath put in their hearts to fulfill His will, and to agree, and give their kingdom unto the beast, until the words of God shall be fulfilled." A change in attitude will occur—from support to hatred and destruction of the whore.

Rev. 17:18 ends by saying, "And the woman which thou sawest, is that great city which reigneth over the kings of the earth." That city is Rome.

Let us consider the location of the crowns on the seven-headed ten-horned beast of Rev. 12, 13, and 17. Crowns on the heads (Rev. 12) represent Rome under the Caesars. Crowns on the horns (Rev. 13) represent Rome at the division of the empire into its ten parts, and specifically Papal Rome. There are no crowns on the beast of Rev. 17. The church is in control of the state.

SECTION 17

REVELATION CHAPTER 18

Rev. 18 is the third repeat of God's judgments on the apostate church—Babylon. Before going into the details of the judgments to befall Babylon (spiritual Babylon), God gives a warning and a call for people to leave the Babylon system, to serve the true and living God.

John sees another angel (a message or messenger) come down from heaven (a message from God). He had great power—the earth was enlightened with his glory. The message would encircle the earth. The message would give light (truth) where the darkness of spiritual error exists.

In verse two, the message from this angel (messenger) is that "...Babylon the great is fallen, is fallen, and is become the habitation of devils, and the hold of every foul spirit, and a cage of every unclean and hateful bird." Brutally frank description of the depths to which the "Christian" world has fallen! It began with perversion of Biblical teaching for the traditions of men; 1 Tim 4:1 says, they will give heed "...to seducing spirits, and doctrines of devils." But as we approach the end, corruptions of all sorts rear its ugly head, and immoral people seem to take the lead even within the confines of the "Christian" church.

Rev. 18:3—The nations have become drunk (spiritually stupefied) by the wine (false doctrines) of her fornications (her departure from Christ, her husband, departure from His word). The kings of the earth have committed fornication with her (Babylon). Spiritual fornication occurs with the kings of the earth when the church links arms with civil governments to enforce her form of doctrines. This usually results, not in spiritual growth of the people, but rather in persecution of those who reject false doctrines enforced by the state.

The latter part of verse 3 says, "...and the merchants of the earth are waxed rich through the <u>abundance of her delicacies</u>." This is the first indication of what Babylon is really like. Babylon is <u>an area of the world filled with delicacies</u> – <u>luxuries</u>.

John hears a voice in verse 4 from heaven saying, "...Come out of her, my people, that ye be not partakers of her sins, and that ye receive not of her plagues." These are the plagues mentioned in the preceding chapter 16. This is the last call to leave the churches of Babylon, teaching error, and to join with the Christian body following closely the truths of the Word of God.

We need to keep in mind that when God deals with a wayward church, His judgments fall on the <u>nation</u> that harbors that church.

The rest of Rev. 18 depicts Babylon as a place overflowing with the luxuries of this world. It does not take much skewing of the imagination to picture Western Europe, the seat of the mother church, and the United States of America (the seat of Protestantism) as meeting the description of the prophecy.

Rev. 18:7 says, "...she hath glorified herself, and lived deliciously." The following verse says, her plagues would come in one day (a day for a year). Four things are mentioned in the plague 1) death 2) mourning 3) famine 4) fire.

Rev. 18:9 says, "...the kings of the earth who have committed fornication and lived deliciously with her, shall bewail her, and lament for her, when they shall see the smoke of her burning." This sounds like the nations supporting the religious Babylon system have traded widely in the earth and have made foreign countries quite wealthy. The downfall of Babylon causes a collapse of trading nations. They will bewail the collapse of Babylon "...for in one hour is thy judgment come." Why will the merchants of the earth weep and mourn? No man buyeth their merchandise any more."

The luxury of Babylon is given in the verses that follow. Gold and silver, precious stones, pearls, fine linen, purple, silk, scarlet, thyine wood, ivory, precious wood, brass, iron, marble, cinnamon, odours, ointments, frankincense, wine, oil, fine flour, wheat, beast, sheep, horses, chariots and slaves.

The prophecy says, these things will depart from Babylon and the merchants who traded with her and who were made rich by such trade shall "...stand afar off for the fear of her torment."

They will lament that this great Babylon which was "...clothed in fine linen, and purple and scarlet, and decked with gold and precious stones, and pearls!" has in one hour come to naught.

Rev. 18:17 speaks of the great overseas trading of Babylon. The shipmasters and those trading by the sea will cry out at the fall of Babylon. Verse 19 speaks of those who were made rich by trading with ships. They will all cry out when Babylon falls.

John sees a mighty angel take up a great millstone casting it into the sea. He says, this is how Babylon will fall and would be found no more at all.

Luxuries of Babylon again are mentioned in verses 22 & 23. They include harpers, musicians, pipers, trumpeters, craftsmen, wedding participants, merchants, etc.

Could these two areas of the world, Western Europe and The United States of America, be headed for God's judgments, in the form of economic collapse from which there will be no recovery?

The prophecy is again reiterated. When this country shall repudiate its constitution as a Protestant and Republican form of government and shall make provisions for enforcing the papal Sabbath (that is Sunday) God will consider this nation to be in national apostasy <u>and national apostasy will be followed by national ruin!</u>

REVELATION CHAPTER 19

Rev. 18 gives us only a partial account of God's judgments on apostate Christianity. More is yet to come. Rev. 19 1–10 is a vision John sees of the saved in heaven. This is an encouragement to God's people before the horrors of Armageddon and the final destruction of the wicked are recorded.

John heard a great voice of many people in heaven saying "Alleluia; salvation, and glory, and honour, and power, unto our Lord and God. For true and righteous are His judgments; for He hath judged the great whore, which did corrupt the earth with her fornications, and hath avenged the blood of His servants at her hand."

In verse 3 again they said, "Alleluia." In verse four the 24 elders and the four beasts (living creatures) said "Amen; Alleluia." In verse six, a great multitude thunders, "Alleluia; for the Lord God omnipotent reigneth."

Rev. 19:7–9 speaks of the marriage of the Lamb, "Blessed are they which are called unto the marriage supper of the Lamb."

Then in verse 10, John fell at the feet of the angel to worship. The angel forbade John from doing that. He told John that he was his fellow servant and of his brethren that have the testimony of Jesus. The angel advised worship God. If angels are not to be worshipped why are millions advised to worship Mary and "canonized saints?" Only God is to be worshipped. The angel then defines what the testimony of Jesus is. The angel said, "...the testimony of Jesus is the spirit of prophecy." In Rev. 22:9

the angel again says, "…I am thy fellow servant and of thy brethren the <u>prophets</u>." In other words the testimony of Jesus is the gift of prophecy.

In Rev. 12:17, the true church of God will keep the commandments of God—all, including the seventh-day Sabbath. James 2:10 says, "For whosoever shall keep the whole law, and yet offend in one point, he is guilty of all." The true church will also have in its midst, the testimony of Jesus which is the gift of prophecy. The Seventh-day Adventist church is the only church in all Christendom which meets all the specifications of the prophecy—the commandments of God and the prophetic gift.

John is then given a vision of the final day of the Lord. In Rev. 19:11–21, he sees the beginning of what is the battle of Armageddon. Revelation is written in symbolic language and the symbols must be related to reality. As we read these texts we are looking towards a reality that we must accept by faith. None of us have seen this planet surrounded by celestial beings before. We believe these things will happen because God's word is reliable. The battle described here is incomprehensibly uneven. John sees "…heaven opened and behold a white horse." The One sitting on the horse is called Faithful and True. This is Jesus who is faithful and true and he judges, and His judgments are righteous.

John describes Him as having eyes as a flame of fire. He had on His head many crowns. His clothes were dipped in blood. He is also called the Word of God. We recall John 1:14 where Jesus is spoken of as the Word made flesh.

John sees the armies of heaven (the angels) following Jesus on white horses.

John sees Jesus with a sharp sword proceeding from His mouth. With that sword He would smite the nations. On Jesus' vesture and on his thigh was written King of Kings and Lord of Lords.

These verses present a symbolic picture of Jesus' return to this earth as promised. John 14:2, 3 reads, "…I go to prepare a place for you. And if I go and prepare a place for you, I will come again, and receive you unto Myself; that where I am, there ye may be also."

In *Daniel's Difficulties Resolved* and in *Revelation's Secrets Revealed* we have taken symbolic prophecies and related them to historic reality. In symbolic prophecy relating to the second coming of Christ, we are relating these to events that the human family has never experienced.

In Rev. 19:17,18 John sees "...an angel standing in the sun; and he cried with a loud voice, saying to all the fowls that fly in the midst of heaven, Come and gather yourselves together unto the supper of the great God; that ye may eat the flesh of kings, and the flesh of captains, and the flesh of mighty men, and the flesh of horses, and of them that sit on them, and the flesh of all men, free and bond, both small and great." These two verses are brought to reality in verse 21.

The great Battle of Armageddon, "fought" on the great day of the Lord begins in Rev. 19. This is no ordinary battle. Symbolically "...the beast, and the kings of the earth, and their armies gathered together to make war against Him that sat on the horse, and against His army." Literal earthly armies cannot fight Jesus symbolically riding a white horse in the heavens. The beast of Rev. 13:1–10 (Catholicism) for centuries has been fighting God in the heavens by doctrines unbiblical and by traditions wholly man made. The verse is simply saying that the beast and the kings of the earth are out of harmony with the King of Kings and Lord of Lords of the universe.

How does this battle end? When Jesus returns the second time Rev. 19:20, 21 takes place. The beast (Catholicism) and the false prophet (apostate Protestantism) will be cast alive into a lake of fire burning with brimstone. They are consumed. "And the remnant..." who are the remnant? We recall that the world of the unsaved are divided into three groups 1) dragon-pagan religions 2) beast-Catholicism 3) false prophet. The beast and the false prophet are consumed in a lake of fire burning with brimstone; the "remnant" is what is left of the three—the dragon power, or the pagan non-Christian religions of the world. These are "...slain with the sword of Him that sat upon the horse which sword proceeded out of His mouth; and all the fowls were filled with their flesh." This last verse fulfills the call made to the fowls that fly (verse 17 & 18) to come and eat the flesh of Kings, captains, mighty men, horses etc. All are consumed, dragon, beast and false prophet. None are left.

The question should be raised, where do God's faithful people fit into this picture? 1 Thess. 4:16, 17 gives us the answer. "For the Lord Himself shall descend from heaven with a shout, with the voice of the archangel, and with the trump of God; and the dead in Christ shall rise first; then we which are alive and remain shall be caught up together with them in the clouds, to meet the Lord in the air; and so shall we ever be with the Lord."

No, secret rapture here! No seven years of tribulation here! No second chance here! No "antichrist" in the middle of seven years of tribulation here! A straight forward second coming of our Lord Jesus; a resurrection of the righteous dead; the righteous living changed in a moment "...in the twinkling of an eye" (1 Cor. 15:51, 52) and are caught up with the resurrected righteous dead to meet the Lord in the air. The beast and the false prophet cast into a lake of fire burning with brimstone; the dragon power slain by the sword of Him that sat on the horse—Rev. 19:21; destroyed "...with the brightness of His coming." 2 Thess. 2:8. This sets the stage for Rev. 20.

SECTION 19

REVELATION CHAPTER 20

Rev. chapters 19:11–21 and 20 are one. The last verse of Rev. 19 finds the world void of people. John sees an angel from heaven come down to earth. He has the key of the bottomless pit. The term "bottomless pit" is used to indicate things that have their origin with Satan. It is also used to refer to this world in a chaotic uninhabited state. The angel had a great chain in his hand.

He laid hold of the dragon, Satan, and bound him a thousand years. How was Satan bound "...that he should deceive the nations no more, till the thousand years should be fulfilled; and after that he must be loosed a little season?" Rev. 19:20,21 sets the stage for this. Satan cannot deceive the nations during the 1000 years for they are dead. It says, "...he should deceive the nations no more till the 1000 years should be fulfilled." What happens at the end of the 1000 years that loosens Satan from his bound condition? Rev. 20:7 says, "And when the thousand years are expired, Satan shall be loosed out of his prison." How is he loosed out of his prison? Rev. 20:5 says, "But the rest of the dead lived not again until the thousand years were finished." The wicked are all slain at the second coming of our Lord. They remain dead during the thousand years. The second resurrection (the resurrection of the wicked) occurs at the end of the thousand years.

In Rev. 20:4 we have a picture of what goes on in heaven during the thousand years. Judgment is given to the redeemed. That judgment is a review of God's dealing with the lost. God has already determined that they are lost. It would be our privilege to review and agree with the justice of God in excluding the wicked.

In Rev. 20:6 a blessing is pronounced on those who had a part in the first resurrection. This occurs at the second coming of our Lord—the beginning of the 1000 years. On these there will be no second death. They will reign with Christ during the thousand years.

After the thousand years are over, the second resurrection occurs and Satan can again deceive the nations which are in the four quarters of the earth. The term "Gog" and "Magog" are used to represent the vast multitude of the resurrected wicked of all ages. John says, they are as the "...sand of the sea." Who is "Gog" and who is "Magog?"

We turn to Eze. 39:1,3,4 "Therefore, thou son of man prophesy against Gog, and say, thus saith the Lord God; Behold, I am against thee, O Gog, the chief prince of Mesheck and Tubal...I will smite the bow out of thy left hand, and will cause thine arrows to fall out of thy right hand, Thou shalt fall upon the mountains of Israel, thou, and all thy bands, and the people that is with thee; I will give thee unto the ravenous birds of every sort, and to the beasts of the field to be devoured." Gog, then, corresponds to the dragon power of Rev. 19:21—the remnant who were slain by the sword of Him that sat on the horse "...and all the fowls were filled with their flesh."

Eze. 39:6 goes on to say, "and I will send a fire on Magog..." Magog, then, corresponds to the beast and the false prophet of Rev. 19:20, who were destroyed by fire.

Gog is paganism. Magog is Christianized paganism. They are dealt with differently at the second coming of our Lord, before the millennium. After the thousand years, both groups are destroyed in the lake of fire which surrounds the holy city.

After the thousand years are ended, the second resurrection occurs. Billions of the wicked of all ages come to life. They are "...as the sands of the sea." The holy city, the New Jerusalem, descends from heaven. Rev. 21:2 & 3 records John's vision of

121

this great event, "And I, John, saw the holy city, New Jerusalem, coming down from God out of heaven, prepared as a bride adorned for her husband. And I heard a great voice out of heaven, saying, behold, the tabernacle of God is with men, and He will dwell with them, and they shall be His people, and God Himself shall be with them, and be their God."

We go back to Rev. 20:9 where it says, the billions resurrected at the end of the thousand years "...went up on the breath of the earth, and compassed the camp of the saints about and the beloved city; and fire came down from God out of heaven, and devoured them."

This is the fire of the last days which rids the world of sin forever. Rev. 20:10 says, "And the devil that deceived them was cast into the lake of fire and brimstone where the beast and the false prophet are." This fire consumes Satan and his followers, root and branch forever. The rest of this verse says, "...and shall be tormented day and night forever and ever." This portion of the verse is used erroneously to teach an eternal burning hell fire. The first concept that needs clarification is that hell's fire is <u>different</u> from the fires we know today. If someone is burnt in fire today he soon becomes unconscious after excruciating pain. He is then consumed—brought to ashes by the fire. The fires of God's judgment are <u>different</u>! God is a God of justice. Justice is effected when the punishment fits the crime—no more, nor no less. If the punishment exceeds what the crime deserves, injustice has occurred. If the punishment does not equal that which the crime deserves, then again injustice has occurred. Only God can fairly determine when justice has been met. In the fires of hell as long as there is material for the fire to prey upon, the person will be aware of it. For many wicked individuals they may thus be tormented days and nights before they are eventually consumed. The "...for ever and ever," indicates that this annihilation is permanent, even as Sodom and Gomorrha were destroyed by "eternal fire," and that fire is not burning today.

In vision, John's attention is now directed back in time to see the process of judgment of the wicked that took place before they were destroyed in the lake of fire. In Rev. 20:11 John sees a great white throne and One sitting on it. The One sitting on it was probably Jesus, for in his own words in John 5:22 he said, "For the Father judgeth no man, but hath committed all judgment unto the Son." Rev. 20:12 goes on to say, "And I saw the dead, (the wicked dead) small and great, stand before God; (not a literal standing before God for they are dead—they stand before Him in judgment) and the books were opened: and another book was opened, which is the book of life: and the dead were judged out of those things which were written in the books, according to their works." Verse 13 adds, "and the sea gave up the dead which were in it; and death and hell (or the grave) delivered up the dead which were in them: and they were judged every man according to their works."

No one can hide; no one will escape the judgment of Jesus in the matter of eternal life or eternal death.

The book of life is mentioned in verse 12. We call attention to the scriptural teaching that all whose names are not found in the book of life will be lost.

Those who have accepted Jesus will find their names entered into the book of life. When probation closes one of two things take place in heaven with the professed followers of Christ.

Rev. 3:5 says, "he that overcometh, the same shall be clothed in white raiment and I will not blot out his name out of the book of life…"

In Acts 3:19, Peter says, "Repent ye therefore, and be converted, that your sins may be blotted out when the times of refreshing shall come from the presence of the Lord."

What these two texts are saying is that either your sins are blotted out and you are saved or your name once entered in the book of life will be blotted out and you are lost. It pays to be faithful to our Lord that our names will be retained in the book of life.

Rev. 20 ends with verses 14 & 15, "and death and hell were cast into the lake of fire. This is the second death." All who are lost die at least twice. "And whosoever was not found written in the book of life was cast into the lake of fire."

Thus ends Rev. 20 and the history of sin.

SECTION 20

REVELATION CHAPTER 21

In chapter 21 John sees a new heaven and a new earth; the first heaven and the first earth were passed away. John, projected in vision, sees the promise fulfilled. In Isa. 65:17 Jesus says, "For, behold I create new heavens and a new earth; and the former shall not be remembered nor come into mind."

We on this isolated planet have a tendency to think of sin as our local earthly problem. We need a broader view and concept of the problem of sin. Sin began in heaven, right in the presence of God and around His throne. That information is given clearly to us in Isa. 14 and Eze. 28. The knowledge of this rebellion spread quickly throughout the vast recesses of God's universe. The plan to rid the universe of sin was made before the foundation of this world was laid. (See 1 Peter 1:20). Our theologians know all the intricacies of the plan of salvation as it pertains to our world. But do we see the bigger picture of how sin has affected God's universe? God will make not only a new earth, but a new heaven also. 2 Peter 3:13 agrees with the promise given in Isaiah, "...we...look for a new heaven and a new earth..."

Jesus speaking through Paul in Heb. 12:26 says, "...yet once more I shake not the earth only, but also heaven"

2 Peter 3:10 says, "But the day of the Lord will come as a thief in the night; in the which the heavens shall pass away with a great noise..."

From these texts it seems to say, that God will reconstruct His entire universe when the sin problem is finally put away.

In Rev. 21:2 John "...saw the holy city, New Jerusalem, coming down from God out of heaven..." Zechariah gives us a picture of what will happen at the end. Zech. 14:4 says, "And His feet shall stand in that day upon the Mount of Olives, which is before Jerusalem on the East, and the Mount of Olives shall cleave in the midst thereof towards the East and towards the West, and there shall be a very great valley; and half of the mountain shall remove towards the North, and half of it towards the South." And verse 9 says, "and the Lord shall be king over all the earth; in that day shall there be one Lord, and His name one." At that time all the promises and prophecies concerning spiritual Israel will be fulfilled and will come to pass.

Rev. 21:3 and on tells the exciting reason why a new heaven is promised. "...the tabernacle of God is with men, and He will dwell with them, and they shall be His people. And God Himself shall be with them, and be their God."

There will be no more tears; there will be no more death; no sorrow nor crying. No pain to mar our happiness.

Again in Rev. 21:5 God says, "...Behold, I make all things new." Apparently God's dwelling with us shifts the center of His universe to where He will dwell with the redeemed.

Without life, all values cease. God says in verse 6 "I will give unto him that is athirst of the fountain of the water of life freely."

And in the following verse, "He that overcometh shall inherit all things." In Rom 8:17, "and if children, then heirs; heirs of God, and joint-heirs with Christ."

John gets a second view of the descent of the holy city. One of the angels who had the seven vials called John to see the bride, the Lamb's wife. He was taken to a high mountain where he saw again, the holy city, the New Jerusalem descending out of heaven from God.

From Rev. 21:11 to 27 John describes the city. It had the glory of God. It appeared as a jasper stone. It had a high wall; and twelve gates with the names of the twelve tribes written thereon.

The wall of the city had twelve foundations with the names of the twelve apostles written thereon. The city was then measured and found to be 375 miles on each side. The building of the wall was of jasper, the city itself was of pure gold. The foundations of the wall were garnished with precious stones. These are listed in verses 19 and 20. The gates were made of pearl, and the streets were of transparent gold!

There was no temple seen in heaven. God the Father and Jesus are the temple of it. The temple (or sanctuary) as described in Leviticus and Hebrews was for the purpose of showing how God deals with the sin problem—those who would be lost (Ps. 73:3–17) and those who would be saved (Ps. 77:13, 15).

The city would not need the light of the sun nor moon. God's glory lightened it. The Lamb, Jesus, was also the light of it.

Apparently, there is continuous light throughout the day. It says, "...For there shall be no night there." This solves a problem on Sabbath keeping in the new earth. Isa. 66:23 says, "...from one Sabbath to another, shall all flesh come to worship before me, saith the Lord." With continuous daylight, time can be the same for every point on the surface of a round world. Every one can be at the place of worship at the same time.

The chapter ends with the assurance that only those whose names are written in the Lamb's book of life will be there.

SECTION 21

REVELATION CHAPTER 22

John continues in vision. The angel shows him "…a pure river of water of life, clear as crystal…" coming from the throne of God and the Lamb. Apparently there is a street also coming from the throne of God. It appears to be very wide. In the middle of the street is the tree of life. The river apparently runs in the midst of the street also with the tree of life on either side of the river. The description is of a trunk rising on either side of the river uniting above into the singular tree of life. It bears twelve types of fruit, one each month. The leaves are for the healing of the nations. As one evangelist puts it, why would healing be necessary in heaven? There would be no sickness there. The human family was injured, in a way, at the tower of Babel. Would the leaves be used to restore harmony and understanding in the human family? We do not know.

Rev. 22:3 assures us again that the throne of God and of the Lamb shall be there and we will serve Him there.

Again in verse 5 we are told that there will be no night there. There would not be the need of the sun. Our light comes from the perpetual presence of the Lord with us. We shall reign for ever and ever. We recall Rev. 1:6 and Rev. 5:10 where the saved would be made kings and priests unto God.

Rev. 22:6 assures us that the words of this book are "…faithful and true." Jesus then speaks, "Behold I come quickly." Time to a God who exists in eternity is not reckoned as we do. A day is as a thousand years and a thousand years as one day. (2 Peter 3:8).

John was so awe-inspired with what he was shown that he fell at the feet of the angel to worship. The angel then forbad him from doing so, saying that he was as John's fellow servant, the prophets. Again is heard the admonition, "Worship God." If people would only obey the injunction given here! Millions would be brought to their senses! No worshipping of Mary; no worshipping of saints! No running to grottos, tree stumps, and the like to view the likeness of Mary! Worship God and God alone!

We backtrack in time again in verse 11, "He that is unjust, let him be unjust still; and he which is filthy, let him be filthy still; and he that is righteous, let him be righteous still; and he that is holy, let him be holy still." When this proclamation goes forth in heaven, it applies to the entire world of the living. Probation is then closed on the world of the living.

Shortly after this, Jesus says, "And, behold, I come quickly; and my reward is with me, to give every man according as his works shall be."

Probationary time is still open on the world of the living, but none know when the fateful words of Rev. 22:11 go forth.

What is the reward that Jesus speaks of when he returns? Is it eternal life? Eternal life is not a reward; it is a gift. However, rewards are given according to the works performed in the Lord's service.

Again, as we find throughout the scriptures, is a call to keep God's commandments, "…that they may have right to the tree of life, and may enter in through the gates into the city."

In verse 16, Jesus speaks, "I Jesus have sent mine angel to testify unto you these things in the churches. I am the root and offspring of David, and the bright and morning star."

Jesus is the root of David—the creator of David. He is also the offspring (of the line) of David. God in human flesh! Wonderful mystery! But it is the truth that sets us free!

The invitation follows, "And the Spirit and the bride say, Come. And let him that heareth say, Come. And let him that is athirst come. And whosoever will, let him take the water of life freely."

Then the warning that if any man should add unto the prophecy, God will add unto him the plagues that are written in the book; and if any man should take away from the word of the book God will take away his part out of the book of life, and out of the holy city, and from the things written in the book.

Then the assurance again, "Surely I come quickly." And the benediction, "Amen. Even so, come, Lord Jesus. The grace of our Lord Jesus Christ be with you all. Amen."

And so ends this commentary on the books of Daniel and The Revelation. As mentioned at the beginning, it is not the intention of the author to deal with every verse in these books. For the purpose of clarity comments on many verses are omitted. The reader is referred to *The Prophecies of Daniel and The Revelation* by Uriah Smith for verse by verse commentary on these books.

May the Lord add His blessing to the reading of His word.

We'd love to send you a free catalog of titles we publish or even hear your thoughts, reactions, criticism, about things you did or didn't like about this
or any other book we publish.

Just contact us at:

www.TEACHServices.com